FRANCIS
BRETT YOUNG

The Border Lines Series

Series Editor: John Powell Ward

FRANCIS BRETT YOUNG

Michael Hall

Border Lines Series Editor
John Powell Ward

seren

seren is the book imprint of
Poetry Wales Press Ltd
Wyndham Street, Bridgend
CF31 1EF Wales

A CIP record for this book is available at the
British Library CIP Office

ISBN 1-85411-208-2
1-85411-209-0 paperback

*The publisher acknowledges the financial support of the
Arts Council of Wales*

Printed in Palatino by
WBC Book Manufacturers, Bridgend

Contents

List of Illustrations

One: Foundations

When, at the end of the nineteenth century, Francis Brett Young surveyed the world from Worcestershire's Clent Hills, he courted a vision which would remain with him for the rest of his life. From just before the First World War, until just after the Second, his literary output was impressive in scope and quality. The magic of the world which he had seen, and anticipated beyond its horizon, took him from the long-established traditions of his home county to the birth-pangs of South Africa. Thirty novels and four volumes of short stories, in nearly two hundred different editions, ranged from fantasy to history, from shocker to moral tale, through adventure and nostalgia, but always back to reality. His prose showed him to be a gifted and careful craftsman, renowned for graceful and delicate descriptions, a quality which only a poet could readily achieve.

His fascination with the English poets began with Shenstone, a fellow son of Hales Owen, expanded throughout the eighteenth century, and was fuelled by the newly-discovered Traherne. Brett Young's own three collections of poetry, written during the two world wars and represented in more than fifty magazines and anthologies, occasionally achieved majestic and haunting lines, and spoke in a lyrical voice of England. An early taste for the classics and the writings of Scott and Dickens fostered an admiration for heroic virtues. His mother's love of music was inherited by the young Francis, whose piano settings of poems by Bridges, Trench and Stevenson were amongst his earliest publications.

Three works of non-fiction, three published plays (with others performed) and miscellaneous further writing in poetry and prose, fact and fiction completed the Brett Young canon. This, however, was only a small part of the picture. From the beginning of his career, regarded as one of most promising new writers, Francis Brett Young excited the admiration of a vast readership from a variety of backgrounds. Often the preferred author of Prime Minister Baldwin, Brett Young was a literary giant in the 1930s, whose novels were found more than almost any other on the bookshelves of the reading public. A consistent bestseller in the inter-war years, achieving sales of half-a-million for his most popular works, his novels were turned into successful films, broadcast on radio and translated into eleven languages, from Norwegian to Spanish, his characters and places being recognised on both sides of the Atlantic.

As a corollary to popularity, criticism followed, carrying with it the stolid and sterile evisceration of his writings by literary intellectuals who possessed little imagination, but great malice. An author who had failed to stand the test of time, Brett Young, critics pronounced, had rightly fallen from fashion. The traditional values which he represented and the lyrical style in which he wrote, were no longer popular. His novels were over-long, repetitious and humourless. He had contrived pale and sentimental characters, smug and comfortable plots. Not a truly creative writer, he only wrote of events and places he knew, and only described people from his own perspective. For his admirers, who read his novels in their thousands, it was in such personal observation and intimate experience that his talent lay, and that an abiding impression was made.

Brett Young, said the critics, lacked originality, blazed no new trails and accepted the status quo. Certainly he was paternalistic toward the native Africans and other foreigners whom he met in *Marching on Tanga*. Assuredly he was patriotic to the point of jingoism, proclaiming his belief in the essential quality and permanence of England in *The Island*. Without doubt, he was anti-Semitic in both fact and fiction. As Shakespeare conformed with the morality of his day, and St Paul uttered no condemnation of slavery, it was perhaps unreasonable to require from Brett Young a larger vision.

Lengthy novels had been the choice of the nineteenth century. Walpole followed suit: *The Bright Pavilions* exceeded seven hundred pages and *Vanessa* was more than eight hundred. Brett Young was condemned for adopting too leisurely a style. In his spacious tales of English countryside and African history, written in measured and gracious prose, he rarely missed a descriptive opportunity, at times allowing his fondness for landscape and occasion to grow more detailed than they might have been. However, his narratives rarely got out of hand, because they were carefully planned, with not only the total length decided in advance, but also the number of words to be allotted to each part of the story. As his novels grew lengthier, so did the critics' complaints. Yet despite their leisurely style, his stories contained a surprising amount of action, having a vital energy all of their own.

Librarians who labelled the latest Brett Young novel as the same story under a different title, were not lacking in evidence in their charge of repetition. Having found the winning formula, Francis was not reticent concerning its re-use. The Town Hall, Council House and Art Gallery of North Bromwich were described by both David Wilden and John Bradley (see Appendix One). The problems of hire-purchase and jerry-built houses were experienced by the Henshalls and the Penningtons. House-bound invalids, Jeffrey Kenar, Mrs Maples and Miss Loach, commented on life beyond their windows. At the beginning, middle and end of his career, Francis employed the imagery of a lion roaring after its prey to describe the volume of church organ music in Brixham, Monk's Norton and Halesby. *A Man About the House* developed the plot of the short story 'A Busman's Holiday', whilst both *Undergrowth* and *The House Under The Water* dealt with the building of dams.

If repetition were regarded as sufficient grounds for disregarding an author, English Literature would be seriously depleted. The consequences of mistaken identity were frequently exploited by Shakespeare; the reader's sympathy was constantly aroused by the plight of Dickens' ill-treated, orphaned heroes; the search for husbands by Austen's marriageable heroines permeated all her writing.

Critics pronounced that Brett Young had no sense of humour, occasionally allowing that even though he might move and touch the reader, he had no capacity for promoting laughter. Though he evidently did not espouse the farce of his fellow Black Countryman, Jerome, sparkling cameos of wit interspersed Brett Young's writing. The assistant who glided across Madame Allbright's dress shop, modelling a black lace evening dress and Dr Medhurst's Medical Decalogue, adopting, as a last resort, one Winchester quart mixture of *God Only Knows*, were both undoubtedly and pointedly humorous.

In spite of the breadth of his understanding of human nature, Brett Young was frequently accused of drawing disappointing two-dimensional characters: mere cardboard cut-outs. Such criticism has been particularly applied to his second-rank characters, often seen as superficial caricatures, rather than discrete personalities, whilst his main characters have been dismissed as failing to arouse the reader's long-term interest. Though there may obviously be instances where both accusations are true, as generalisations they are unjust and unfair.

Used partly as a commentary upon the fickleness of society, with its changing attitudes to those values which it once held dear, Captain Small, who first appeared as a somewhat pathetic, chain-smoking, whisky-swilling old soldier, existing purely on past glories, did not develop predictably. Though the fall from grace of the heroine whom he had idolised almost destroyed him, Captain Small actually grew in stature, as he sought some new bedrock on which to stand. Neither might the stern, but just, Dr Weir, respected by patients and neighbours alike for his kindly generosity, be regarded as flat or colourless. As Captain Small grew, so Dr Weir diminished, compelling his granddaughter (who had embraced the religion which he despised) to read aloud lubricious accounts of the Oxford Movement, in which he took a prurient delight. Finally, in a fit of pique, he disinherited her. Not much hint of cardboard here.

With minor characters Brett Young succeeded in painting, in a few words, both people in whose company the reader would spend a delightful hour and those whom he would cross the road to avoid. With major characters, his books left an aftertaste. Would· the Pennington's marriage survive? How would Abner Fellows fare in the army? Characters remained on the reader's conscience, their significance continued to fascinate, long after the story ended.

Perhaps the most consistent criticism levelled against Francis Brett Young was that his writing was unrealistic and anodyne; that though his stories may have been vividly told, he never completely entered into the sharp actualities of life, but presented its hardships from a safe and detached distance. Thus the reader was never really involved, but was offered instead a pleasant and comfortable escape into self-deception and nostalgia. Certainly his writing inclined to the calm and serene rather than the melodramatic; certainly there were traces of whimsical charm and mellow grace. But it is only part of the duty of literature to confront and challenge: it should also have the power to comfort and uplift.

Simply because he loved more than he despised, encouraged more than he discouraged, and wrote honestly, unencumbered by false sentiment, Brett Young frequently raised the reader's imagination to the world where it longed to be. That is not to say that his stories failed to confront. Dr Bradley coped with: the youthful struggle against ignorance and poverty; his father fatally injured by a rogue horse; his daughter stillborn; his wife killed by a virus which he himself had brought home; his son on the verge of manhood, the victim of the drug-addiction which claimed his life; his sole friend killed by an infection contracted from a patient; his fortune lost in the Sedgebury Main Colliery disaster. Abandoned by her father, following the death of her mother, Bella Small was expelled from school as ungovernable, and unjustly dismissed from work as a threat to her employer's son's honour. Unexpectedly inheriting a fortune, she squandered it, capriciously restoring the house with which she had become obsessed. The death of her husband in the Boer War and her son in the Great War, and the destruction of the house by fire, finally resulted in Bella abandoning her dream and seeking happiness away from the scene of her loss.

Such heroes and heroines faced the realities of the world in which they lived: not always a comfortable or escapist world. Homelessness and unemployment, family breakdown and poverty, drug abuse and debt, none of which were either unrealistic or anodyne, were brought into sharp focus, as the writer took an in-depth look at the characters and situations he had created. Francis Brett Young was a convincing story-teller, who possessed the ability to tell an agreeable and interesting tale at length; to make his characters change and grow; to linger over scenes and landscapes, often the chief protagonists in his dramas; and to communicate his own vivid sense of place to his readers.

Before he was a writer, Brett Young was also a doctor, the accuracy of whose observation could be seen whether he was describing the raw drama of the horse-breaking which cost Matt Bradley his life, or the social niceties of afternoon tea in Jane Weston's drawing room. Houses and places were of immense importance to Brett Young, who had an eye for marrying landscape with incident. Frequently he made use of lengthy descriptions of scenery with close attention to topographical detail, setting his characters against backgrounds of towns and workshops, hills, rivers and mountains. The actions and adventures of his characters illuminated the landscape, as when Abner Fellows lost his way whilst carrying Gladys Malpas over the hills from Brampton Bryan to Wolfpits, or when Jenny Badger, pushing a perambulator, followed the meanders of the River Teme.

Fundamentally a poet before he was a novelist, Brett Young's inclination was always to poetry rather than prose, even though his poetry may more often have been implicit in his novels than explicit in his verse. His prose, marked by a contemplative and reflective style, was also suffused, even in scenes of intense action or industrial violence, with a quiet and gentle atmosphere which only a romantic poet could create. Combining the warmth and vision of the poet with the precision and clarity of the doctor, in all that he wrote Brett Young was a meticulous craftsman, who employed a rich vocabulary and worked with a deliberate artistry to produce tranquil and leisurely stories of even texture, which were usually extremely well-constructed. With versatility, melody and grace and yet with an undoubted technical accomplishment, he revelled in colour, action and adventure to create, both in broad sweeps and in fine detail, the aura and spirit of his chosen world.

Like Scott, who introduced Charles II and Titus Oates into *Peveril of the Peak*, it was part of Brett Young's technical accomplishment to weave into his imaginary world historical events, such as the 1901 Birmingham riot which threatened Lloyd George's safety, and real characters, such as Cecil Rhodes and Dr Jameson, making it difficult to tell where fact ended and fiction began. Within his world, the lives of his schoolboys and lovers, soldiers and doctors, iron-masters and nail-workers, country squires and village parsons, together composed into one cohesive panorama, in which people, places and events were all linked.

Brett Young's stories of Worcestershire, the Welsh Marches and the Black Country, sometimes called his Mercian novels, covered a wide time-span, from the Franco-Prussian War of 1870 up to the period immediately before the outbreak of the Second World War. The web which together they spun, created something of a saga of life throughout this period of rapid change. However, this borderlands saga was not like Trollope's *Palliser* novels or Galsworthy's *Forsyte* series, in which stories followed one after another in chronological sequence. Brett Young's books did not need to be read in any particular order. In general, each covered the same period, telling of characters who came to the front and then disappeared, only to reappear unexpectedly in other novels, as in real life, as the panorama of human destiny unfolded within the chosen landscape.

The enjoyment of more than one existence in Brett Young's little world, both by characters whose histories occupied whole novels and those whose cameo appearances featured only in supporting or background roles, did much to bring his stories to life.

Mr Ingleby, whose chemist's shop was a feature of Halesby in the early years of the twentieth century appeared both in *The Young Physician* and in *My Brother Jonathan*. Jonathan's father was a patient of Dr Verdon in *Wistanslow*. Jonathan himself, who completed his medical training in the book which bore his name, was called out to assist in an emergency in *Dr Bradley Remembers*. Dudley and Ernest Wilburn, the North Bromwich solicitors who acted for Dr Weir and his family in *Portrait of Clare*, also acted for the Tinsleys in *White Ladies*. The firm remained active in the 1930s, serving John Bulgin in *Mr & Mrs Pennington*, in which Ernest Wilburn's suicide, so devastating in both earlier novels, still haunted. The character of Alaric Grosmont, clerk in Wilburns' offices, was fully developed in *The Dark Tower*. David Wilden of *Far Forest* worked in the same Great Mawne Colliery as Abner Fellows of *The Black Diamond*. Abner's dog, Tiger, was shot by Farmer Cookson who also appeared in *This Little World*.

That Brett Young was not always accurate in the details of the lives he created for his characters was illustrated by North Bromwich doctor James Altrincham-Harris, already with thirty years' experience when Edwin Ingleby worked with him in *The Young Physician*. A generation later, when giving evidence at the Inquest into the death of Solomon Magnus, the same doctor informed the coroner that he had been a medical practitioner for thirty-five years. Perhaps including a doctor in a novel was more important to Dr Brett Young than getting the details right. When Jim Redlake collapsed at Trewern he was attended by Dr Hendry, whilst a few years later, Susan Pennington was attended by Dr Hendrie following her accident at nearby Chapel Green: surely too much of a coincidence for this to be any other than the same medic with a name that the author had only vaguely remembered.

It was not only the reappearance of characters, but also of places and events which added realism to an imaginary world, for Brett Young was not content to paint a believable cast against a shadowy background. The limited landscape in which the novels were set, guaranteed the repeated existence of cities such as North Bromwich, towns such as Halesby and villages such as Chapel Green. More subtly, backdrops were created to make their own distinctive contributions to the shaping of saga and community, linking returning characters with familiar places and well-rehearsed events.

Brunston Public School, of which Dick Pennington was so proud, was the very academy to which Matthew Bradley also won a scholarship. Edwin Ingleby, Jonathan Dakers and John Bradley all walked the wards of Prince's Hospital. The incense of Alvaston's High Anglican chapel of St Jude was savoured by both Clare Lydiatt and Ellen Isit. Jasper Mortimer, Joseph Hingston and Walter Willis gained their fortunes in the profits which industry reaped from a succession of wars. Catherine Weir, Eugene Dakers, Griffith Tregaron and John Bradley lost their fortunes in the disastrous flooding of Sedgebury Main Colliery.

Perhaps it was attention to apparent trivia which best made plain the reality and continuity of the world which Brett Young had created. The significance of the policeman on point duty in Sackville Row, holding up the traffic to allow Susan Pennington to cross the road was only fully developed nine novels later, when Owen Lucton returned to North Bromwich after his adventure. Then it was the successor to that earlier policeman who held up the Sackville Row traffic and permitted Mr Lucton to cross, and the reader saw that in detail such as this, Francis Brett Young's world came to life.

The world of the Mercian novels was a comparatively little one. *Undergrowth* and *The House Under The Water* were located at one end of the pipeline of the Birmingham water scheme, *The Iron Age* and *The Young Physician* at the other. For the detail with which he created this carefully delineated and vibrant little world, Brett Young earned the label of regional novelist. Certainly, the great majority of his novels dealt, either wholly or partly, with one clearly-defined geographical region and its inhabitants, throughout a crowded and tumultuous sixty years of history. Within these parameters he wrote solid, traditional stories of the West Midlands and the Welsh borders.

Brett Young lived in an age when the regional novel was a popular genre. With the publication of *Far From The Madding Crowd* in 1874, Hardy had resurrected the ancient name of Wessex for his extended Dorset, and translated Dorchester into Casterbridge. In the *Clayhanger* series, which appeared between 1910 and 1918, Bennett depicted life in the Potteries, which he called the *Five Towns*. Close contemporaries of Brett Young were Mary Webb, whose *Precious Bane* (1924), one of a series of novels celebrating rustic life in Shropshire, became an instant best-seller when praised by Stanley Baldwin, and Winifred Holtby, whose real-life portrait of the workings of a Yorkshire County Council appeared in *South Riding*, awarded the James Tait Black Memorial Prize in 1936.

Elements of the style of each of these writers may be found in Brett Young's regional novels. The hardship of the everyday lives of Hardy's country folk was recreated in the nailers, chain-makers and miners who inhabited the poorer quarters of Brett Young's world. Whereas Hardy's people were often pitted against a malignant fate, which ruled and destroyed their lives, Brett Young's remarkably resilient characters rarely succumbed to the hardships which surrounded them, but confronted their destinies in ordinary circumstances, which, though often depressing, sordid and squalid, did not preclude the leading of heroic lives. Bennett's picture of the rise of an avaricious manufacturing class in Victorian England, with the consequent exploitation of the dependent working class was reworked in the lively portraits of Brett Young's integrated manufacturing concerns of the Black Country, where aspiring owners rose on the backs of middle-men and cottage workers. The detailed accounts of business and public affairs drawn by Holtby, were echoes of the hospital committees of Brett Young's novels. Added to all this was a romanticism less naive than that of Webb, with which Brett Young feelingly and vividly evoked the Worcestershire countryside, introducing its charms to a vast and appreciative public.

Adopting a style common to writers of regional novels, Francis Brett Young gave names to the places of his imaginary world which were often only thin disguises for their originals. Birmingham became North Bromwich and its suburb of Edgbaston, Alvaston. Hales Owen was changed to Halesby and Hawne to Mawne, whilst Clent Hill was renamed Pen Beacon and Walton Hill, Uffdown. Dudley, the capital of the Black Country, was rechristened Dulston, and the neighbouring town of Stourbridge, Stourford. Chapel Green and Lesswardine were the Chapel Lawn and Leintwardine of Herefordshire; Monk's Norton was an amalgam of Worcestershire villages, Chaddesbourne D'Abitot somewhere near Chaddesley Corbett, and Wolverbury was not quite Wolverhampton.

However, Francis Brett Young was far more than a regional novelist. *Sea Horses* and many of the short stories of *Cotswold Honey* proved that he was equally adept at creating settings, both harsh and romantic, on sea as well as land. Sometimes his world spread far beyond the confines of the borderlands which terminated at each end of the Birmingham to Elan Valley pipeline. Novels were set, either wholly or partly in Leicestershire, where his Cold Orton, Essendine and Thorpe Folville respectively interpreted the villages of Cold Overton, Whissendine and Somerby; in Somerset, where Rowberrow was changed to Highberrow; on Salisbury Plain, where Pedworth was his chosen name for Tidworth; in Devon, where the back streets of Brixham were described in *Deep Sea* just as graphically as the slums of North Bromwich in *The Young Physician*; in London, of suffragettes and aristocracy, of Oxford Street and Lupus Street; in the Mediterranean, where he imagined the Republic of *The Red Knight's* Trinacria; in Italy, of *Black Roses* and *A Man About the House*; and in Africa.

As the Mercian novels introduced Worcestershire to the reading public, so *Pilgrim's Rest* and *Woodsmoke*, and especially *They Seek a Country* and *The City of Gold* (which unlike the Mercian novels were developed chronologically), by their expert blending of fact and fiction, did much to interpret the history of modern South Africa to a wide audience. The hundreds of scenes and scores of characters crowded into these South African novels demonstrated the writer's versatility, for Brett Young wrote with the same skill equally of humble English country folk and pioneers in Africa. Indeed they could well be of the very same stock, linked by their creator's fascination with the mass movements of communities, whether it were the Great Trek of South Africa's founding fathers, the repeated waves of immigration and emigration which determined British history in *The Island*, or the annual migration of Black Country hop-pickers from the oppressive industry of their home towns into the more desirable rural farmlands of Worcestershire.

At the end of the nineteenth century, Hales Owen, Francis Brett Young's birthplace, was at the meeting point of the two worlds of industry and agriculture and the conflict between black and green was a constant theme of his writing. As he would make the transition from one world to another, progressing from Hales Owen to Fladbury, so many of his characters made the same journey, symbolic of that from despair to hope. The obvious setting of unwholesome urban materialism against rustic rural virtue, often involving the encroachment of the works of man upon unspoilt nature, aided and abetted by the ambitions of the nouveau riche and resisted by the impoverished aristocracy, featured in many novels, raising issues of ecology and environment before their time had come. More than that, the conflict of black versus green was used by Brett Young as a vehicle for other issues which concerned him. Novels with medical backgrounds particularly addressed the fight between disease and health. *The Crescent Moon* dealt with the conflict of savagery versus civilization, whilst that of slavery against freedom occupied many of his heroes, who sought to throw off the ties which bound them to labour, land or routine. Thus black versus green was, for Brett Young, an appropriate imagery for the unending struggle between darkness and light, ugliness and beauty: a vivid picture of the eternal quest for truth.

The juxtaposition of Hales Owen between the black and the green, and the changing times about which he wrote, provided much of the inspiration for Brett Young's novels. His world was one of agricultural depression; of the decline of the old land-owning families of the shires; of the end of the hand-made nail trade; of the collapse of the vast integrated coal and iron industries; of the replacing of horse and carriage by cycle and car. The lives of his Halesby characters held in tension the conflict between the industrial Black Country, the ever-increasing metropolis of Birmingham, and the Worcestershire countryside. The way in which these worlds related to each other fascinated Brett Young, who set out to write entertaining stories about ordinary folk, which revealed how they lived, the kind of things they did and the ways in which they were influenced by their environment. So the world of which he wrote was one, not of imagination, but of experience, in which men and women from every walk of life, the rich and successful as well as workers in factory, field and mine, appeared.

Perhaps Brett Young was at his best when dealing with people at work: his writing certainly displayed a detailed knowledge of the livelihoods and habits of widely separated social groups, for he dealt not only with the employers and gentry to whose society he aspired, or the professional class to which he first belonged, but also with the colliers, ironworkers and labourers who had been patients at his father's surgery. Thus, in his novels, appeared clergymen, doctors, lawyers and teachers, soldiers and shop-keepers, farmers, financiers and fishermen, makers of bricks, chains and nails, casual labourers and domestic servants, managing directors and union activists, hop-pickers and miners, iron-masters and land-owners.

To careful study and observation, to which his training as a doctor and experience as a writer encouraged him, Brett Young brought an artist's insight. His feeling for history, interest in character and meticulous concern for detail, were complemented by a poetic sense of imagination, which enabled him to write with sensitivity about the daily lives of a whole range of people and the environmental influences which affected them, from the coal mines of the Black Country to the diamond mines of the Rand. Such were the skills which put flesh on the bones of history: an ability to write descriptive passages which revealed an awareness of the demographic, economic and social background of his world, against which the thoughts and actions, foibles and uncertainties, successes and hardships of his characters were set.

In vivid descriptions of the Black Country, in pictures of Worcestershire countryside, in stories of the new commercial aristocracies of Birmingham, and in landscapes, enriched by a whole variety of human experience beyond the borderlands, were contained Brett Young's own particular vision and reflections upon it. The abiding importance of his novels was that they painted a unique picture, in which depth, colour and substance brought to life the statistics, reports, documents, ledgers and minutes which he had undoubtedly studied, but which, without the poet's vision, remained arid. Poet, physician and novelist, whatever his theme, Brett Young treated it with careful study and close observation, and presented the results in a clear and graceful style.

His skill in bringing the past to life guaranteed that his novels would endure. Though Francis Brett Young may not have been a great writer, he was certainly a good one. A romantic and a realist, his novels provided impressive and intimate insights into the habits, outlook, lifestyle and social conditions of the late nineteenth and early twentieth centuries. His ability to see the ordinary, everyday things which others saw, but transform them, by his poet's touch, into distinctive stories rich in atmosphere, gave him a uniquely individual voice, providing vivid insights into the world of which he wrote: a world which no longer exists.

However, the writings of Francis Brett Young were not just concerned with resurrecting a dead and forgotten past, for they dealt with the great and timeless themes of life and death, love and hate, risk and endeavour. Contained within the paragraphs of his prose and the stanzas of his verse was the whole gambit of the tragi-comedy of human life. The collective story which he unfolded illuminated fundamental and universal truths, and illustrated his power to handle the peaks and troughs of life, as well as the plains. There were not always happy endings; but neither was hope always abandoned, nor joy frustrated. The scenes which he observed and the tales which he told were always interesting in their own right; but more than that, they illuminated a larger truth and a broader theme, common to all literature of abiding worth.

In their quest for fulfilment, both material and spiritual, Brett Young's characters were seen at work and at leisure, in times of war and peace. For the young, school days sometimes proved unbearable. Edwin Ingleby's life at St Luke's was hardly more happy than that which Dickens envisaged for David Copperfield at Salem House. Family life was examined and sibling rivalry explored. The problems which addressed the extended family of Adam Wilden covered the same conflicting interests as those which faced the home of Sir Thomas Bertram in Austen's *Mansfield Park*. The exploits of Charlotte Bronte's Robert and Louis Moore in *Shirley* anticipated those of Jonathan and Harold Dakers. Happiness was grasped and lost. The drunken debauchery of John Fellows devastated his home as surely as did that of Arthur Huntingdon in Anne Bronte's *The Tenant of Wildfell Hall*. New relationships developed. The eternal triangle of young love, in which Susan Pennington's liaison with Harry Levison almost destroyed her marriage, was a rather more sordid version of Glencora Palliser's dalliance with Burgo Fitzgerald in Trollope's *Can You Forgive Her?* The mutual love and concern of Adrian and Jacoba Prinsloo throughout all the exigencies of married life, reflected, more tenderly, that of Captain and Mrs Booth in Fielding's *Amelia*. As courtship faded into marriage, Gabrielle Hewish's domination by Marmaduke Considine was as much a tragedy as was Dorothea Brooke's by Mr Casaubon in Elliot's *Middlemarch*.

Wealth and poverty were united in marriage. Bella Tinsley's fortune was used to restore the neglected home of the impoverished Hugo Pomfret, as Soames Forsyte had Robin Hill built for the penniless Irene Heron in Galsworthy's *The Man of Property*. Fortunes were made and lost. In his parabolic journey through prosperity from the poverty to which he ultimately returned, Griffith Tregaron was a reflection of Michael Henshard in Hardy's *The Mayor of Casterbridge*. Generous and kindly deeds were balanced by deceit and falsehood. The inter-dependent fortunes of such vastly different characters as Robert Bryden and Enrico Massa had been seen before in Becky Sharp and Amelia Sedley of Thackeray's *Vanity Fair*. Sinister characters absorbed oppressive environments. The Grosmonts of *The Dark Tower* and the Furnivals of *Cold Harbour* had lived before in the Earnshaws and Heathcliffs of Emily Bronte's *Wuthering Heights*.

The young looked forward with trepidation and hope, whilst the old looked back with satisfaction and regret. The passing of one age made way for the birth of another; the ambitions of some were achieved; others struggled for justice through suffering and oppression. The journey to a new and better world, where hope offered more than mere survival, which took John Grafton upon the Great Trek, was no less than a secular version of Christian's journey to the Celestial City in Bunyan's *Pilgrim's Progress*. Death appeared in all its guises: in childhood and old age, caused by war and disease; it was sudden and lingering, judicial and self-inflicted, accidental and violent, unexpected and timely. But always it was one of the realities of life, reported not with the cloying sentiment of Dickens, but with all the medical precision with which Gustave Flaubert recounted the death of Emma Bovary.

In the biography which follows, Francis Brett Young's life story is largely told through the experiences of characters (see Appendix One) who, in his imagination, revisited the places which shaped his life. The schooldays, early tribulations and disappointments of his *awakenings* were relived by Edwin Ingleby. Francis's journey from the fringe of the Black Country to the heart of Birmingham, where education would set his foot upon the ladder of *medicine*, was followed by Jonathan Dakers. Life as a ship's doctor, whose voyage took him from Birkenhead to China, was recreated through the narrator of 'Shellis's Reef'. Solace in the *borderlands* of England and Wales, where Brett Young regularly renewed his spirit, was also discovered by Owen Lucton. A medical practice was purchased by Dr Bradley, and life in *Brixham* experienced by Reuben Henshall. East African *war* service with General Smuts was part of Jim Redlake's story, and the economic advantages of life in *Capri* were enjoyed by Hugo Pomfret. When *recognition* allowed Brett Young freedom to select his life-style, he chose a Worcestershire estate and a life similar to that led by the Pomfrets, Ombersleys and D'Abitots of his novels. The happiness and contentment which the final chapter of his life offered him in *Africa* was also discovered by John Grafton.

Unlike Emily Bronte or Walter Scott, in whom imagination counted for more than experience, the story which Francis Brett Young told throughout his novels, short stories, plays and poems, was principally his own life-story; the themes which he developed and the situations which he explored, were those which, in some measure, touched his own life. In part, if not in whole, his stories always derived in plot, setting, circumstance or character, from responses to his own experience, accurately described with all the care and charm of a graceful symphony or delicate water-colour.

After some years of neglect, there are signs of a contemporary rediscovery of the breadth and depth of Brett Young's work. For the first time, he is the subject of entries in both the *Oxford Companion* and the *Cambridge Guide* to English Literature. Extracts from his writings have recently been quoted in learned scientific journals, as well as anthologies of prose and poetry. There is a thriving and enthusiastic Francis Brett Young Society, with a membership drawn from four continents. Neglect may have been an unfortunate historical oversight; rediscovery may be no more than a mere vagary of fashion. It may also be the realisation that again and again, Francis Brett Young took an episode or scene that belonged to one place and time and released it from its parochial setting, pointing up those elements within it that were of universal significance. His world may have been a little one, his horizons limited, his outlook prejudiced, but the truths he examined are of abiding interest, and for that alone, he deserves a lasting place on the shelf of outstanding twentieth century literature.

Two: Awakenings

YOUNG JACKSON: On Monday 11 June 1883 at St Mary's Leicester, Thomas Brett, second son of Thomas and Caroline Young of Rowberrow, Somerset to Annie Elizabeth, middle daughter of John and Sarah Jackson of Somerby, Leicestershire.

Thomas Young, described on his son's marriage certificate as 'gentleman', was descended from Mendip calamine and lead-miners: an isolated and savage folk, whose ignorance and violence induced the novelist-tractarian Hannah More, to mission the area at the end of the eighteenth century. Like others of his ancestors, Young was an accomplished dowser. John Jackson, who by the time of his daughter's marriage was both surgeon and Registrar of Births, Marriages and Deaths for Somerby District, began his career, as did his father and two brothers, as a chemist in Leicester. The financial success of his medical practice enabled him to hunt with the Cottesmore four times a week and to take his place within Leicestershire society.

The newly-married couple made their home at Hales Owen in Worcestershire, where the groom entered general practice, having secured the position of Medical Officer and Public Vaccinator to Romsley District and Bromsgrove Union, eventually becoming Hales Owen's Medical Officer of Health. The Laurels, situated at the very edge of the town in what was then called The Buckhouse, Grange Mill Lane, in which Dr Thomas Brett Young set up his practice, was one of the largest houses in Hales Owen. Its previous occupant had been nail master Edward York, who lived there with his large family and resident servants, an extensive household which Dr Young's would, in time, surpass.

The Laurels was both an attractive and a busy place. In summer, sweet-smelling white jasmine clothed the red brick of the surgery, whilst in autumn the front of the house was covered with virginia creeper. Climbing roses scrambled over wire arches in the garden, which supplied vegetables, apples, strawberries, red and black currants, gooseberries, and parsnips which the cook turned into wine. A large damson tree shaded the fowl pen, from which came new-laid eggs, and nearby stood the greenhouse where tomatoes were grown. The larger of two yards housed the stables where the doctor kept two ponies and a trap, the essential means of communication with his patients.

Indoors, the drawing room, with its many ornaments, housed a Bechstein piano, whilst in the dining room, alongside encyclopaedias, a tall bookcase contained the novels of Dickens and Scott. A corridor led to the surgery, with separate waiting rooms for private and public patients; the doctor's consulting room, connected by a speaking tube to the main bedroom on the first floor; and the dispensary, where the medicine bottles which had been washed in the back yard, were filled, neatly wrapped in white paper and sealed with red sealing-wax. Also on the first floor was the room destined to become the schoolroom.

At The Laurels, on the evening of Sunday 29 June, 1884, Annie gave birth to her first child, Francis Brett Young. The middle name 'Brett', which having received himself, Thomas Brett Young would bestow on all eleven of his children, was the maiden name of his mother Caroline Brett, of Hoddesdon in Hertfordshire. An earlier Caroline was the source of Francis Brett Young's earliest memory and earliest dreams.

> In the room where I slept as a child hung a worsted sampler, a map of Africa, made in the year 1820 by a certain Caroline Brett.
> (FBY 32)

A similar tapestry in Jim Redlake's bedroom served the same purpose in first sounding the call of Africa.

> A sampler hung on the wall, representing the continent of Africa. It had been made in the year of Waterloo, by a great-great-aunt. Above its pink-coloured Southern extremity it was embroidered in black, as a reminder that the whole of its uncharted centre was abandoned to heathen savagery.
> (JR 36-37)

On Sunday 24 August 1884, at the Parish Church of St John the Baptist, Hales Owen, where his father would later be churchwarden, and which he would christen 'our little cathedral', Francis Brett Young was baptised by Rev. Charles Nation, five days before his birth was actually registered, his father incurring the 7/6d fee then in force for those who did not register a birth within six weeks. For seven years Francis was an only child, his mother miscarrying three or four times before his sister Doris was born in 1891. A brother, Eric, was born in 1893 and a second sister, Joyce, in 1895. In addition to the family, The Laurels accommodated a resident housemaid and, when there was a new baby, a monthly nurse. Medical students, who assisted Dr Young in the practice, were taken as boarders. During these years of early childhood, Francis was inevitably spoilt, especially by his mother, whom he called 'Honnie', and whose pet name for him was 'Tim'. His lifelong pleasure in music and literature was instilled by 'Honnie', who played Beethoven and Mendelssohn on the drawing room piano and read the novels of Charles Dickens from the dining room bookcase. Thus a lasting seasonal pleasure was generated. 'My mother used to read Dickens's Christmas Books aloud to me about Christmastide and I've found pleasure in reading them myself at this time ever since' (FBY 185).

Scenes and illustrations from these early years, both significant and trivial, find their place in Brett Young's novels, as fiction, genealogy and history are interwoven. Beatrice Ingleby and Elizabeth Redlake, mothers of two of his heroes, both had two sisters, the eldest of whom died in childbirth, the youngest of whom was doted upon by parents. The forebears of John Ingleby, who earned his living as the Halesby chemist, were the very Mendip miners who had resisted the evangelism aimed at their salvation.

> At Highberrow in my father's cottage, there were only two books: the bible and a tract by Hannah More. She made the Mendip miners notorious by trying to convert them. Neither she nor her influences would ever have converted your grandfather.
> (YP 182, 176)

Like Francis's grandfather, Edwin Ingleby's grandfather was a dowser, a necessary member of his community. 'In a dry country like Mendip the dowser is most important; for neither man nor beast can live without water, and he is the only person who can tell where a well should be sunk' (YP 177). Dr Bradley and Dr Verdon both had speaking tubes from their surgery doors to their bedrooms and Dr

Bradley was instructed when dispensing medicine to 'wrap it up neatly with a nice, smooth fold down the back of the bottle and a well-written label' (DBR 243). It was a monthly nurse who gave information concerning his mother's illness to Edwin, who remained the only child that Francis had been for so long. 'His mother had expected to have a baby-sister for him, and before the first jealousy that had flamed up into his mind had died away, she told him how the baby had been born dead' (YP 27). Mrs Verdon and Mrs Ingleby both found release from their burdens by playing the piano, Mrs Verdon's music being 'as much an attribute of herself as the scents of her favourite flowers: an infinite avenue of escape from the narrow conditions of life in a small town on the verge of the Black Country', (W 3) whilst Mrs Ingleby made the ornaments on the piano dance, when she played Beethoven's 'Sonata Appassionata'. Edwin's school holidays were regularly made more pleasant when his mother read aloud to him from the novels of Sir Walter Scott.

Amongst the most significant influences in Brett Young's early life was his grandfather, whom he recalled with great affection.

> Dr Jackson of Somerby, a staunch Gladstonian Liberal and a free-thinker, drove me day after day over the rolling grassy upland of gated roads by Whissendine, Knossington, Cold Overton and Ashby Folville. His was the principal influence of those early days: a brave and good man, universally respected and (what is more important) universally loved.
> (FBY 2594)

Jim Redlake's grandfather, Dr Weston of Thorpe Folville was also 'a Gladstonian Liberal and (though he read the lessons in church) a free thinker' (JR 47). Day after day Jim accompanied him in the dogcart along the lanes of High Leicestershire to Essendine, Ross-ington and Cold Orton, dismounting from the trap to open gates and meeting the villagers whose affection for Dr Weston was as obvious as was that of the members of the hunt with which he rode. In the idyllic setting of Thorpe Folville, Jim learned to ride, as his creator, during the long summer holidays, had enjoyed rides in the country on one of his grandfather's hunters. The cobbled yard in which Dr Weston stabled his horses and the kitchen garden in which his vegetables were grown were reminiscent of those at The Laurels.

When at home, Francis occupied his spare time cultivating the hobby which would endure: fishing, in the millpond at the end of the lane and Shut Mill pool near Walton Hill. Edwin Ingleby enjoyed the same hobby in similar locations, seeking 'the silvery roach of the millpool and the mythical carnivorous pike lurking in Mr Willis's ponds in the Holloway' (YP 165).

From The Laurels, Brett Young looked out upon the Clent Hills, which he would capture in his writing as 'Pen Beacon heaving its fleece of black firs, and the domed head of Uffdown', (YP 32) a sight which excited his imagination and gave him his earliest inspiration. What at first was unattainable soon became the destination of boyhood cycle rides.

> In the early years before I had climbed the Clent range, I made the lands beyond them the scene of all my imaginary adventures: the jungles in which great beasts were slain, the fields on which battles were fought, and indeed, the whole kingdom which the people of whom I had read in books, inhabited. Then, one summer day, I was taken to the crown of Walton for a picnic and saw below me all the kingdoms of the earth.
> (FBY 23)

Subsequently Francis was to inform E.G. Twitchett, his first major literary critic, that from the top of Walton could be seen the whole world about which he wrote. The boy who enjoyed the outdoor life, who collected butterflies, birds eggs and fossils, and who had an annoying habit of sniffing, also had ambitions to be a poet; aspirations which he allowed Edwin Ingleby and Richard Verdon to share.

> I had just discovered the poems of William Shenstone and learnt that he had been born and bred in Halesby. His was the only 'great' name that my birthplace had ever produced; his memorials were a small marble urn in the church, a dilapidated tomb in the graveyard, and a public-house in the Stourford Road.
> (W 16-17)

From Shenstone both Francis and Edwin turned first to other minor poets of the eighteenth century, Akenside, Dyer and Lyttelton, before progressing to Tennyson's *Idylls of the King* and the rather more sensuous Keats; Longfellow, however, irritated. Shenstone is perhaps remembered more for his landscape gardening than his poetry, and it was at The Leasowes above Hales Owen that the youthful Francis Brett Young 'scribbled verses and declaimed them to trees that an idealised (unworthily perhaps) poet planted' (FBY 186).

In 1891, the year in which Doris was born, Francis was sent to Iona Cottage High School in Sutton Coldfield. Separated from his family, he was lonely and homesick and found it difficult to relate to other pupils, who did not find him particularly attractive. At Iona, already the victim of the tension-induced migraines that were to dog his adult footsteps, and already prone to day-dreaming, Francis met his first experience of bullying, both mental and physical. His inability to concentrate meant that his chair was placed close to the teacher's desk. There he would sit, gazing abstractedly at the ceiling, lost in some imaginary world, until brought back to reality by a sharp rap on the head. These were not generally happy years for Francis, who covered his self-conscious shyness by raising a cordon of critical scorn, the occasional reappearance of which would protect him for the rest of his life.

Iona was typical of the many small preparatory schools established in uneconomical, rambling houses, this one having narrowly escaped demolition for the railway line which crossed the Birmingham to Lichfield road near Sutton town centre. The joint principals were sisters, Mary and Susie Cull: Mary, delicate and extremely irritable, the donor of the many slaps which Francis received; Susie, understanding and generous, the donor of Stevenson's *Black Arrow* for Francis's birthday. Their elderly mother, a great favourite with the pupils, baked the home-made bread which formed part of the Iona diet. The curriculum was unexceptional: much rote-learning of set passages and interminable long-division sums. More imaginatively, there were organised walks and drives in the park, as well as the dancing classes at a nearby hotel, where Francis, though suffering torments of shyness, encountered 'a little, sallow girl, who kindled a flame both hot and passionate. An ugly little girl, on reflection, with very long hair and very short legs. But the first!' (FBY 2655).

Already showing talent as a violinist, Francis played Tollhurst's 'Reverie' as a solo at an end-of-term concert for parents, leading Miss Susie Cull to the opinion that his obvious artistic aptitude would find its fulfilment in music. However it was an out-of-school activity which claimed Francis's greatest interest, sowing the seeds of future literary development.

.   My private sanctuary was the banks of a little stream at the

bottom of the Tamworth Road. There I indulged my passion
for running water, constructing in sand and mud, enormous
works of hydraulic engineering, staging naval battles, wrecks
and tempests, absorbed and utterly happy.
(FBY 2655)

Brett Young's recollections of these early school days were fleetingly reborn when Matthew Bradley who, like his creator, played
the violin and suffered from 'sick headaches that crushed and paralysed him with agonizing pain for twelve hours at a stretch' (DBR
395) was sent to 'a preparatory school in Sutton Vesey, on the
Staffordshire side of North Bromwich' (DBR 393). In the creation of
fictional town names, Brett Young drew the flimsiest veil of disguise.
The principal benefactor of Sutton Coldfield, which lies to the North
East of Birmingham, was John Harman, the sixteenth century Bishop
of Exeter, who adopted the name, 'Vesey'.

Before taking up the violin, Matthew Bradley had learned to play
the piano. With Francis it was the other way round. In his teenage
years he taught himself to play the piano, his first tune being 'Mary
was a Housemaid'.

Epsom College, to which Francis won an entrance scholarship in
1895, was more than fleetingly described in *The Young Physician*.
Here Epsom, which had opened forty years earlier as the Royal
Medical Benevolent College, was re-christened St Luke's. To this
establishment Edwin Ingleby was awarded an entrance scholarship
also in 1895, and his experiences for the next six years were very
much those of his creator. Accompanied by his mother as far as
London, Victoria, Edwin made the rest of the journey alone and
arrived at the school in the throes of a migraine. From his first day
he was homesick and bullied by the established pupils who regarded him as an easy victim.

Isolation weighed heavily upon Edwin. He didn't wish to be
different from others, although he felt that his mind was of a
painfully foreign texture. He knew that things somehow
struck him differently. Edwin longed to be normal, and they
wouldn't let him.
(YP 12)

Francis entered Carr House, and though Edwin's house was never
identified, the association was established through the studious

head prefect of Edwin's house, whose name was Carr. Unhappily, Ingleby remained the isolated target of schoolboy cruelty, until he eventually made friends with a pupil who shared the name of Widdup with two brothers who entered Epsom College in the years before and after Brett Young. A period of relative calm then followed for Edwin. 'He shook down into his proper place in the scheme of things and nobody took much notice of him' (YP 17). Presumably the same was true for Francis Brett Young, of whom nothing was heard in school records for four years after his arrival at Epsom. In May 1899, he was elected to the debating society, of which he became an active member, speaking in favour of war in the Transvaal and against government support for hospitals and professional sport. Obviously a successful orator, the only debate in which he was defeated was that in which he opposed the motion that 'science is a better foundation for education than classics'. In a school which had been established for the sons of doctors, this was hardly surprising. Brett Young carried the day in a debate about working women, with his view that women were made for man's comfort not his support, a piece of male chauvinism which would be only partly contradicted in his own marriage.

An early indication both of the high regard in which Brett Young held duty to country, and of the love which he would develop for the history of South Africa, is suggested by his choice of Kipling's 'The Absent-minded Beggar' as his contribution to a school literary evening in November 1899. Just over a year later, his musical talents were employed in a house competition when, anticipating a role which would occupy his leisure-time in Brixham, he conducted the Carr Quartet singing 'Evening' by O.C. Martin and the Glee Group in 'Fairies' by Walter MacFarren. Carr House came second and the headmaster commented on the role of the conductor, who could generally secure the trophy.

Encouraged by the affable Mr Cleaver, form-master of the Lower Fifth and former cricket 'blue', Edwin Ingleby, who had not been a great success at games, never having played competitive sports before, 'found himself becoming keen on cricket. Little by little he conceived an interest in the progress of his own County, Worcestershire, in those days slowly rising to fame' (YP 44-45). Brett Young's interest in the game and the county team, which also developed from his days at public school, remained an abiding fascination wherever he lived.

The boy who was a dreamer at Iona Cottage High School positively cultivated this talent during history lessons at Epsom and spent his spare time voraciously reading books borrowed from the school library. For this, Edwin Ingleby, who was attracted at an early stage to the bookcase that contained the poets, was criticised by his headmaster. 'Ingleby, you're a dreamer. There's no use for dreamers in this world. They're not wanted. Even dreamers with the blessing of good brains' (YP 78).

The headmaster of St Luke's, 'a pale man with a lined blackbearded face,' who 'believed in hard games, corporal punishment, nature study and the classics' (YP 78) was an accurate picture of Brett Young's headmaster, Rev. Thomas Hart-Smith, a rigid disciplinarian, a classical scholar and a great naturalist. Other members of staff are also easily recognisable. Tommy Neale, the long-serving mathematics teacher at Epsom, who played the flute in his spare time, became St Luke's mathematics teacher Tommy Heal, who also gave melancholy performances on the flute. Music master Dr Sammy Rowton, the composer of hymns in the Epsom College manuscript book, appeared at St Luke's as Dr Sammy Downton, the composer of 'the chants to which their psalms were sung. At first they were inflicted upon the choir in manuscript; but in Edwin's second summer they appeared collected in a slim grey volume' (YP 46).

During the classics viva of his entrance examination to the University of North Bromwich, Edwin selected a passage from Sophocles and read it 'in the level voice which the Head at St Luke's always used in the recitation of Greek poetry' (YP 231). As classics and English poets were so important to Edwin Ingleby, so, when he looked back upon his time at Epsom, these same treasures were most vividly impressed upon Brett Young's memory.

> I left the school with a love for Latin and Greek, which I owed entirely to the inspiration of Hart-Smith. I did, indeed, know a great deal of Sophocles, Euripides and Aeschylus by heart, together with a mass of Virgil and Catallus besides having saturated myself with English poetry.
> (FBY 2764)

H.V. Plum, M.A. (Oxon), housemaster of Holman from 1897 to 1908, who progressed to the headship of Kelly College and was the original of the sour and disappointed Vincent Perrin in Hugh Walpole's novel *Mr Perrin and Mr Traill*, was also caricatured by Brett

Young as the languid headmaster Kelly of Halesby Grammar School in *The Iron Age*. Mr Kelly, who neither desired contact with his pupils outside school hours, nor believed anything in Halesby to be worth the effort, employed termly reports as his opportunity to invoke private grievances upon his public situation, regretting 'all those mean wasted years at Halesby: the humiliating economies; cold failure unwarmed by any glow of enthusiasm. I haven't a single memory of Oxford worth a halfpenny' (IA 31). In a letter to Martin Secker, written shortly before the publication of *The Iron Age*, Brett Young commented that he had not been so profoundly depressed by Epsom College as had Walpole, who had joined its staff in 1908.

Alongside the staff of Epsom, Brett Young also transferred the college slang to St Luke's. Griffin, Edwin Ingleby's malevolent tormentor, boasted of his liaison with one of the 'skivvies' — the name given to the maids who served in Main Hall; whilst Mr Leeming, form master of the Upper Fourth, was undoubtedly 'pi' — pious and sanctimonious.

It was during his time at Epsom that Francis took the first practical steps in his proposed literary career. During the school holidays he edited *The Laurels Magazine*, produced in the schoolroom of his family home, with contributions from Doris and Eric. In January 1900, he became editor of *The Epsomian*, a commercially-produced publication, in which his editorials were usually introduced by an appropriate quotation.

On the final Founder's Day before he left Epsom, Francis received from the guest of honour, Sir Herbert Maxwell, the first Rosebery Prize for English literature, the only honour which he, who was never head of house or team captain, ever won during his school years. Five years later, Birmingham surgeon Jordan Lloyd, who was considering sending his son to Epsom, sought Brett Young's advice, thus eliciting a final comment on his schooldays.

> 'Is Epsom a good school?' says he. 'The best in England,' I reply, 'but don't send a delicate boy there — it's a rough place.' And so it was, by Jove, in my day.
> (FBY 274)

During Francis Brett Young's adolescent years, three major personal upheavals occurred to disturb his family stability and future plans. The effect of these traumas was to remain with him for the rest of his life and to be repeatedly apparent in his novels.

The first tragedy was the death in 1898 of his mother, at the early age of forty-one, on the eve of Francis's fourteenth birthday. Although partly prepared for the loss by her year-long illness, the blow when it fell was severe. At the end of the nineteenth century, still a generation before the discovery of insulin, only diet could hope to delay the progress of the disease from which she suffered: diabetes, which manifested itself in loss of weight, tiredness and eventually coma and death.

In a cathartic piece of writing, twenty years after the event which moved him so deeply, Francis included in *The Young Physician* the medical symptoms which preceded the death of Mrs Ingleby. After hearing of his mother's frequent tiredness, Edwin commented upon the fact that she seemed much thinner than he remembered, and then noticed that

> she was not allowed to eat the same food as the rest of them. Instead of bread she was ordered to eat a sort of biscuit. 'What are they made of?' he asked; and they told him 'Gluten. That's the sticky part of wheat without starch.'
> (YP 28-29)

Like Francis, Edwin Ingleby was called home from school with the news that his mother was gravely ill. On the journey home he encountered a fellow passenger whose prognosis of his mother's condition was more accurate than sensitive.

> 'Diabetes.... It's a bad complaint. Very. I'm afraid I can't give you the hopes that I'd like to.'
> Edwin couldn't quite suppress a desire to be further informed on certain technical details. 'Is it a painful death?' he asked.
> 'Painful? Well ... not to say painful. Not as painful as some. Most pass away in their sleep.'
> (YP 111)

The diabetic coma into which Edwin discovered his mother had fallen, was identical to the cause of Annie Young's death. It is interesting to speculate whether this concern for medical accuracy was evidence of the hindsight of medical training, or if the youthful Brett Young had already developed (or inherited) an eye for medical detail, which, despite his grief, was both real and intense. The catharsis of *The Young Physician* however, required more than a retelling of medical facts.

In this harrowing autobiographical episode, Francis described the great sorrow, into which he believed no one else, except perhaps his father, might fully enter, which befell Edwin Ingleby, who, at a similar age, endured the loss of his mother. Edwin's Aunt Laura came to stay to look after Mrs Ingleby in her final illness: in reality it was Francis's grandmother, Sarah Jackson, who provided this care. The funeral service at Hales Owen Church, conducted by the rector Canon J.C. Hill, followed by burial in the churchyard, the day after that birthday which was surely the worst in Francis's young life, was the inspiration for mourners who behaved, at best out of morbid curiosity, at worst out of sheer hypocrisy. The red-haired funeral director with one shoulder lower than the other from the constant carrying of coffins, who superintended the burial of Mrs Ingleby in Halesby churchyard (where he also officiated at the interment of Edward Willis's mother in *The Iron Age*) was, in fact, none other than John Jones, the fiery red-bearded undertaker of Hagley Road, described by his granddaughter Lena Schwarz in her history of Brett Young's birthplace, *The Halesowen Story*.

Most telling of all however, was the realisation that with this death came the end of the tenderness and joy which both Francis and Edwin had shared with their mothers. 'All the music and all the beauty that had been there had gone out of the house. The house was an empty shell. Like a dry chrysalis. Like a coffin' (YP 139).

That Edwin's feelings, as well as his experiences, at this traumatic time were a mirror of those of his creator, was made clear in a letter from Francis to his father in October 1919.

> The part you will find most affecting is that which deals with Ingleby's mother's death. That as far as Ingleby's feelings are concerned, is almost a transcript of my own in 1898. It was an episode that affected me more deeply than anything else in my life.
>
> (FBY 567)

As part of the recuperation process Edwin Ingleby accompanied his father on a journey to their Mendip roots, the identical journey to that which Francis and Thomas Brett Young had made in the year following Annie Young's death. Edwin's great-aunt Lydia, who consoled his father that he would get over his loss, even bore the same name as Thomas Brett Young's last-surviving aunt, Lydia Hare, who gave the same assurance to her nephew. Several years later, neither this meeting, nor the loss which occasioned it, had faded from Francis's mind. 'This beautiful old lady told my father he would forget his trouble. Father protested, "No". She said, "Sooner than the boy will". And the boy hasn't forgotten it yet' (FBY 163).

It was not only Edward Willis and Edwin Ingleby in Brett Young's early Mercian novels who had the stability of home and family shaken by the deaths of their mothers, for in this they were joined by Abner Fellows, who did not even remember the event. All three heroes shared a further upheaval in their young lives when their fathers married again: Walter Willis whilst Edward was a pupil at Halesby Grammar School; John Ingleby after Edwin had gone up to North Bromwich Medical School; John Fellows just as Abner's schooldays were coming to an end: in other words, for all three just at a time when, in the nature of adolescent development, they were likely to be most critical of their fathers. For none of the sons was the acquisition of a stepmother a satisfactory experience. In the narration of *The Black Diamond*, where it is legitimate to assume that only the truth will be told, Brett Young affirmed the entire reasonableness of John Fellows' second marriage. 'In spite of Abner's scorn the proceeding was natural enough. The man was under forty, and had been a widower for more than fourteen years' (BD 14). For Abner however, things would never be the same again. Recalling the happy times before his father's second marriage, he could only regret that from the day his stepmother first appeared, his own life became more complicated.

Edwin Ingleby also struggled to admit to himself the reasonableness of his father's action, but could not come to terms with it, neither as it fed his own jealousy, nor as it maligned the memory of his mother.

> He could not define the passionate mixture of resentment, jealousy, shame and even hatred, that overwhelmed him. He admitted it wasn't his business to decide whether his father should marry again or remain a widower. From every point of view the world would conclude that he was doing the correct and obvious thing. However calmly he tried to consider the matter the thought of his mother rose up in his mind: beautiful, pathetic, and indefinitely wronged.
>
> (YP 387-388)

Though apparently less disturbed than either Abner or Edwin by his stepmother, Edward did not enjoy an easy relationship with the second Mrs Willis. She tried to play a mother's part in his upbringing, but failed for lack of understanding and again the truthful narrator observes reality: the father who 'in some departed spring' had married his first wife

> quite forgot that early marriage, for in every direction his life had changed. It was not possible to imagine Edward's mother, so fragile, so girlish in the rather pretentious setting of the later Mawne.
> (IA 20)

When young Matthew learned that his widowed father, John Bradley, had written to Mary Sanders proposing marriage, the consequences were immediate, dramatic and desperate.

> Matthew's cheeks blanched deathly pale: there was no life left in the pallid mask but that of his eyes which continued to stare at his father with a dreadful, malevolent intensity. Then, suddenly, a shocking thing happened. With a swift, convulsive movement his right fist shot out to land with all the strength that was in him on John's defenceless mouth.
> (DBR 478)

John Bradley tore up the letter and the catastrophe was postponed, though the inevitable clash between this father and son would ultimately prove as tragic as that between Sohrab and Rustum in Matthew Arnold's poem.

The second great upheaval in Francis Brett Young's life, which was to mark the end of a domestic chapter, followed hard on the heels of that event in the wider world which would bring to an end the era into which he had been born: the death of Queen Victoria. On 26 February 1901 at Christ Church, Ealing, Dr Thomas Brett Young married again. His second wife was Margaret Allan, the daughter of George Allan who lived for a time at Corngreaves Hall, which was built at the end of the eighteenth century for the Cradley ironmaster James Attwood. Corngreaves Hall was the inspiration for Francis Brett Young's *Mawne Hall*, the home of Walter Willis in *The Iron Age*. Mawne Hall was a saga in its own right: its social events were attended by Edwin Ingleby in *The Young Physician*, by Clare Lydiatt in *Portrait of Clare*, by Jonathan and Harold Dakers in *My Brother Jonathan* and by Owen and Muriel Lucton in *Mr Lucton's Freedom*. In *This Little World* the house was put up for sale and by the time of *Mr & Mrs Pennington* it had been acquired by Solomon Magnus, the North Bromwich stockbroker.

George Allan, who was to become Francis's stepgrandfather, had been the managing director of the enormous Hales Owen-based New British Ironworks, which had gone into voluntary liquidation in 1887. Similar integrated companies (this one dealt with coal, iron, bricks and forgings) such as the associated industries of Josiah Tinsley and Co. Ltd (pivotal in *White Ladies*) featured prominently in Brett Young's writing. When the New British Ironworks was sold in lots in a series of auctions between 1893 and 1897, George Allan became manager of the Corngreaves Furnaces Company, which, as its name suggests, acquired the blast furnaces which had been part of the giant corporation.

Unlike Abner Fellows' father, of whom Francis was later to write in attempted self-convincing mitigation that 'the proceeding was natural enough', Thomas Brett Young was not under forty, had been widowed for less than three years and Francis found it impossible to come to terms with this new domestic arrangement. More than thirty-five years later, in a letter to the Irish playwright and critic St John Ervine (to whom *Mr Lucton's Freedom* would be dedicated), discussing his latest novel, *Dr Bradley Remembers*, Francis used the second marriage of the eponymous hero's mother to show the hurt that still remained from his own similar experience.

> John Bradley was shocked and revolted (I don't say unreason-
> ably) by his mother's second marriage. Wounds of that kind
> go very deep. Though I certainly wasn't the victim of a
> 'mother-fixation' I had no real feelings for my father and I
> could never achieve, or even want, intimacy with him after
> his second marriage.
> (FBY 2713)

It is not difficult to see why those of Brett Young's characters who endured the loss of a natural parent and the acquisition of a step substitute, found the experience to be such an unrewarding one.

The Laurels, at the turn of the century, was not a happy home for the eldest son, who was informed by his father that he was both a constant worry and source of pain. Though Francis apparently tried hard to please Thomas and to heal the rift, he failed dismally. His references to his stepmother as 'Mrs Y' are indicative of the lack of affection between them. Evenings were marked by bitter silences, when the breach between father and son widened and the animosity between stepmother and stepson was rehearsed.

> Father is morose because someone has been praising me to him and it always upsets him by negating his pet ideas. Mrs Y is a trifle more annoying than usual. I don't mind her big 'works of darkness' half as much as her eternal pinpricks.
> (FBY 179,180)

In the harsh judgements which he made in this new relationship, Francis did not stand alone. His brother Eric also displayed a strong antipathy towards his stepmother and a love/hate relationship with his father. Sarah Jackson, too, allied herself with those who did not favour the new Mrs Young and Francis made clear the dilemma in which he was placed, when recounting a visit to his grandmother.

> She filled my mind with sedition, conspiracy and rebellion against the 'lady of the house' of whom she had lately heard several injustices of the grosser sort. I listened, but whatever else I may be, I shall endeavour to be loyal to these people, although I seem to owe them very little happiness.
> (FBY 175)

It was not surprising then, that Francis should have despaired of this period of his life as a time of unending gloom in a house where the atmosphere was not merely lonely, but hostile and suspicious.

Between 1902 and 1908, seven children were born to Margaret and Thomas Brett Young. Though Francis was to enjoy fishing expeditions with his younger stepbrothers and stepsisters of this second marriage, the barriers that divided them were never entirely removed. More than seventy years later, long after Francis's death, the fact that he had resented his father's remarriage and had been jealous of the consequent second family, was still remembered by those who felt themselves to have been unjustifiably disparaged. One younger brother declined to become a member of the *Francis Brett Young Society* on the grounds of the unkindness which he believed that Francis had displayed towards his stepmother. Wounds of that kind certainly do go deep.

In addition to being the year of his father's second marriage, 1901 was also the year of the third bitter sorrow in Francis Brett Young's life. To further his early ambitions to become a writer he had hoped to win a scholarship to Balliol, where he would eventually become a Fellow. His father, however, was determined that Francis would enter the new University of Birmingham to study medicine. The disappointment was relived by three of his heroes. Like their creator, Edward Willis, Edwin Ingleby and Jim Redlake all dreamed of Oxford. Jim had no vocation for medicine, but believed that Balliol would prepare him for a career in writing. Edwin spoke for all three when he imagined a new life of leisure, spaciousness and culture which had become his chief ambition. The dashing of Edward's hopes in his father's simple assertion, 'The boy's my only son. When I'm old he must take my place. I think it's almost time he was beginning, without wasting time at those places', (IA 30) introduced the disappointment of each one. Edward must go straight into the family business; Jim must prepare, not at Oxford but at London, to take over his grandfather's practice; Edwin must accept the fact that finances would not stretch to Oxford, only to North Bromwich, where he would enable his father vicariously to realise some of his own unfulfilled ambitions.

Though Dr Thomas Brett Young had no need to feel that in encouraging his eldest son to enter medical training he was in any way realising any of his old ambitions, he obviously hoped that when qualified, Francis would remain close to home, writing to him in 1907, 'a restrained but kindly letter, very like him and very unlike me. He wants me to go and do hospital posts — with Hales Owen in the background I suppose' (FBY 328).

Like Edward Willis, who remained sulkily submissive at the shattering of his Oxford dreams, Edwin Ingleby and Jim Redlake bowed to the inevitable, as did Francis in his turn. Edwin, however, realised that 'it was going to take all the beauty that he had conceived out of his life. His soul sent forth a cry of exceeding bitterness', (YP 221-222) which must have resembled the cry sent forth by Francis Brett Young's soul at the dashing of his own Balliol dreams, a sorrow still sparking literary recollection more than thirty years later. Filial obedience predominated at the beginning of the twentieth century and Edwin Ingleby, remembering how he had felt at the death of his mother that 'he would do anything in the world to comfort this desolate man, whom he had always taken for granted and never really loved', (YP 130) determined once again to love his father and carry out his wishes. So it was that the first and last of the upheavals of Brett Young's adolescent life merged into one, the enormity of the first only being fully comprehended in the disappointment of the last. 'In Edwin's life the death of his mother had been the point of crisis; but this he had only realised when his hopes of Oxford had been dashed for ever' (YP 241).

As part of his own attempt to rehabilitate his father, or at least show him the love and admiration which were his due, almost twenty years after this sequence of events which had hurt him so deeply, Francis dedicated *The Young Physician* to Thomas Brett Young,

> which is only fitting seeing that but for you I should never have been able to write about the life of a medical student (or for that matter — any life at all). I hope you will find the book interesting and amusing. Also take the dedication for the sincerest part of it.
> (FBY 567)

However, the compliment of the dedication hardly mitigated the rebuke of the story and as a generalisation it is true to say that the fathers of Brett Young's heroes and heroines command little sympathy: not from their offspring; not from other characters who live in their stories; not from the reading public: a fair indication that their creator himself felt as little sympathy for them, as in reality Francis had felt for Thomas. Stepmothers may be the object of scorn or jealousy; natural mothers may fondly indulge their offspring; but it is for fathers that a widespread opprobrium is reserved. Though some fathers hardly appear at all, as in *Portrait of Clare* and *White Ladies*, the reader is left in no doubt as to their lack of paternal feelings.

Having given piano and singing lessons to both young ladies, Ambrose Lydiatt suddenly eloped with Sylvia Weir after showing equal and secret enthusiasm for her sister. Sylvia died in poverty and Lydiatt emigrated to Canada with a new wife, leaving Clare, his daughter, to the mercy of her aunt and grandfather. He is, in short, an irresponsible adventurer. In a similar category came Rupert Small, a draughtsman in the offices of Josiah Tinsley & Co. Bella Mortimer eloped with Small when her father dismissed him on discovering their affair, and died shortly after the birth of their daughter, also named Bella. Small had no feeling for the child and gave her into his parents' care, prior to moving to London, where he met a wealthy widow, whose children were, providentially, almost grown up. Obviously having little interest in these children, Small used the opportunity finally to divest himself of any remaining responsibility for his own child.

> He proposed to abandon Bella entirely if his parents would be good enough to take her off his hands. It would be better, he felt, for both of them since it was not as if the child knew him or cared for him.
> (WL 99)

Other fathers, though remaining in the background, were nevertheless there, either as brooding presence as in *Far Forest*, or flitting in and out of the action as in *Jim Redlake*, but in neither case as influences to be admired or respected and certainly little deserving of love.

Though not deliberately cruel to his children, the Mawne Heath chain-maker Aaron Hadley treated them much as he treated his dogs, alternating between kindness, irritability and complete neglect. After his wife had left home, unable any longer to tolerate his infidelities, 'Bloody Aaron', of whom no good was known throughout the Black Country, decided that he was no longer able or willing to look after his children on his own. When it was suggested that he sent them to his sister-in-law who would care for them, Aaron was only too happy to comply.

> 'But I reckon I'll keep our George,' he added, as an afterthought. The word 'keep' suggested a litter of puppies, the rest of which might be drowned.
> (FF 15-16)

At the beginning of the novel named after his son, George Redlake, the calculating, embittered, egotistical and unsuccessful writer, was anxious to shake off the responsibility of his wife and child, so that he might be free to pursue his literary career. Elizabeth Redlake fled to her parents' home, taking Jim with her. Though George followed, it was not his intention 'to waste time and money by driving out to Thorpe Folville and persisting in an unseemly dispute over the body of a child whom he didn't want' (JR 83). So it was that he passed out of Jim's life, except as a vague impression and a name on a book jacket, which must not be mentioned in the hearing of his formidable grandmother. When father and son eventually met again some years later at the home of a mutual friend, George Redlake first failed to recognise Jim and then continued to speak as though he were not present. A second meeting was quite sufficient for Jim to make the discovery for the first time in his life, that he hated his father.

Still other fathers, though present throughout their children's formative years, were basically self-centred and had their favourites. Though they treated their eldest sons unfairly, their good names were ultimately posthumously preserved by the selfless actions of the very sons whom they had wronged, as in *My Brother Jonathan* and *The House Under The Water*.

The pompous and pretentious Eugene Dakers, so obviously shoddy and ridiculous, was regarded as a joke by everyone except his wife. However it was his third-rate verse, tragic in every sense of the word, which finally provoked Jonathan, the boy whom he habitually neglected in favour of Harold, his younger son, to denounce Eugene as counterfeit and selfish. Death came unexpectedly when the drunken Dakers was involved in a road accident; with it came the revelation that this man of airs and graces was, in real life, nothing more than the impecunious Midland representative of the Fit-U Corset Company. Even worse was the disclosure that the father had misappropriated his elder son's trust fund for his own purposes. Despite all that had happened, Jonathan Dakers with no sign of rancour, determined, at the expense of his own bank balance, to settle his undeserving father's debts.

Tyrannical and blustering, Griffith Tregaron not only alienated friends and neighbours by his overbearing temper, but constantly betrayed his wife by his philandering. He bullied his children, not always unkindly, though their days were undoubtedly lighter when he was absent from home. Each periodic return heralded a new upheaval in family life in which some project over which they had no control was imposed upon them. Rob, the eldest son, was particularly singled out for Tregaron's ire. Though Rob's expertise was essential to the running of the farm, in a fit of pride and pique, like a latter-day King Lear, his father dismissed him when he spoke the truth that Tregaron did not wish to hear. When Tregaron died despised and penniless, it was Rob who, like the equally maligned and ill-used Jonathan Dakers, settled his debts and provided for his stepmother and sister.

Much more sympathy was evoked by John Bradley, the kindly and considerate Black Country doctor, who was deservedly loved and respected by his patients. The story of his half-century of devotion to the people of Sedgebury was very much a biography of Dr Thomas Brett Young, who died at the age of eighty-four in the very year in which *Dr Bradley Remembers* was published. Though as a doctor John Bradley was unquestionably a hero to be admired, the portrait of him as a father was less appealing. Like Francis Brett Young, Matthew Bradley was the victim of severe attacks of migraine for which morphine was prescribed. John Bradley failed to recognise the clues which should have been obvious to any doctor, that his son had become a drug addict. Tragically, Matthew died of an overdose, the reader being well aware that the real causes of the addiction were rooted in his unhappiness and the misguided expectations of his father. This was a death which could have been avoided if only the father-son relationship had been happier and Matthew allowed to follow his own course, which would have lead to classics at Oxford, rather than medicine at North Bromwich simply to fulfil his father's selfishly vicarious ambitions.

Thus it might reasonably be concluded that even where tragedy was avoided and the young people whose stories were told in these novels enjoyed a happy home life, it was little thanks to their fathers, with whom their relationships, if they existed at all, were at least as strained as those of Francis Brett Young with his own father.

Three: Medicine

In 1901, succumbing to parental pressure, Francis Brett Young went up to the new University of Birmingham, which had received its charter in the previous year. The medical faculty, in the old Mason College, was located in the city centre. It was at forerunners of this institution that Thomas Brett Young (who entered Queen's College in 1875) and Francis's grandfather, John Jackson, and great uncle, Jabez Bunting Jackson, (who both entered Sydenham College in the 1850s) had received their training. The School of Medicine in Birmingham owed its origins to William Sands Cox, the founder of both Queen's College and the Queen's Hospital. Cox, who lectured in anatomy, physiology and pathology, funded the first medical lecture rooms and library out of his own pocket, eventually having an entrance scholarship named in his honour. It was with a Sands Cox Scholarship (valued at forty-two pounds per annum) that Francis Brett Young entered the University, his conviction that he had been plunged neck-deep into medicine before he was seventeen, giving a clue to his frame of mind. In his father's presentation copy of Windle and Hillhouse's history *The Birmingham School of Medicine*, Francis would have been able to read of a midwifery colleague of William Sands Cox called John Ingleby — the very name which he was to borrow for a central role in *The Young Physician*.

Both students initially lived at home and the daily train journeys made from Hales Owen to Birmingham by Francis Brett Young in his early university days were repeated in those of Edwin Ingleby. At the beginning of the twentieth century the line from Birmingham to Stourbridge connected with the five-minute journey on the busy Great Western Railway from Old Hill to Hales Owen, where the station master, H.W. Payton, lovingly tended the gardens which bordered his platforms. Edwin looked out upon the stark contrast between Hales Owen and the neglected Black Country which, like his creator, he left behind on passing through Haden Hill tunnel.

> The train journey from North Bromwich lay through a vast basin of imprisoned smoke, bounded by hills dominated by the high smoke-stacks of collieries, many of them ruined and deserted. At a dirty junction he changed into the local train, its carriages old and grimy. Through a short but sulphurous tunnel the train emerged into the valley of the Stour: the vista of the hills unfolded, and later the spire of Halesby church appeared at the valley's head.
> (YP 242-243)

Had either Francis or Edwin still been making this journey at the end of their university days, they may have noticed improvement at least in the means of transport, as in 1905 a third-class only rail motor-car service with new rolling-stock was introduced on the line between Hales Owen and Old Hill. However, with his second-class season-ticket and opportunity for regular observation, Edwin Ingleby was more interested in his fellow-passengers:

> a youth articled to a solicitor in North Bromwich; a gentleman with a bloated complexion and a fawn-coloured bowler hat, reputed to be a commercial traveller; a superior person with a gruff voice who was a clerk in a bank in the city; and a withered man of fifty who travelled into North Bromwich daily on some business connected with brass. Naturally there were more interesting people on the main line than on the Halesby branch.
> (YP 247-249)

Lena Schwarz provided the evidence that the passengers with whom Edwin travelled on his daily journey included those with whom Francis had made the journey at the identical period of his life. The 'withered man of fifty' who travelled daily into North Bromwich 'on some business connected with brass' was none other than Brett Young's regular travelling companion from Hales Owen to Birmingham, John Brookes, who was enraged to recognise himself.

Independent evidence of the 'more interesting people on the main line' was provided in the autobiography of Brierley Hill business-man, J.N. Hickman, then a railway goods clerk working for G.W.R. at Hockley, and one of the passengers whom Francis Brett Young regularly joined on the second stage of his daily ride from Old Hill to Birmingham. Along with Hickman, Fred Fisher (a fellow Birmingham medical student) and an unnamed passenger, Brett Young frequently spent the journey in games of solo whist. Though there were no card-playing medics who travelled with Ingleby, there were certainly a pair of clerks, one at least a young man in training; the unknown passenger allows the reader freedom of imagination; and the 'withered man of fifty' has already been firmly identified.

Further contemporary evidence of those distant salad days was provided by Hales Owen industrialist and local historian, Frank Somers, at whose wedding Francis would be best man. Somers was a metallurgical student at Birmingham when Brett Young was reading medicine and the two young men frequently made the most of their meagre allowances by sharing lunch at Joe Hillman's Restaurant in Hill Street. First established in neighbouring premises in 1862, Joe Hillman's was very much a male preserve, providing a meeting place both for Birmingham's Musical Society and Shakespeare Reading Club. This, in addition to its affordable prices, made it just the sort of place where students aspiring to the culture which Brett Young and Somers evidently sought, might congregate. Here, for metallurgist and medic, lunch often consisted of half a pint of beer with cheese and new bread, and a Brett Young story thrown in. Edwin Ingleby whose tastes were largely those of his creator, found similar delight in a place of similar name.

> Joey's was an institution of some antiquity, opposite to the Corinthian Town Hall. It was a long and noisy bar at which, for the sum of fourpence, one consumed a quarter of the top of a cottage loaf, a tangle of water-cress, a hunk of Cheddar cheese, and a tankard of beer.
> (YP 263)

Brett Young entered into a range of student activities: playing full back for the university rugby team; reading papers on Charles Kingsley and the 'Mission of Poetry' at meetings of the Medical Literary Society, which had been founded by Dr William Wright a lecturer in anatomy (who appeared in *The Young Physician* as Dr Robert Moon); and joining the editorial board of the university magazine, *The Mermaid*. Allowed similar interests, Edwin Ingleby found a place in the scrum of the second fifteen and read a paper on Thomas Browne's *Religio Medici* at the Literary Society of which he became a member. It was at a meeting of the Medical Literary Society that Brett Young first met Humphrey Humphreys and laid the basis of a friendship which would last for the rest of his life. Together with six other like-minded medical students, Brett Young and Humphreys formed a group known as the Octette, sharing a common interest in literature and music; together attending concerts in Birmingham and opera in London; spending free weekends cycling and walking in the country and making the first tentative attempts at artistic creation.

The founder of the Octette was Lionel Chattock Hayes, to whom Brett Young would dedicate *The Iron Age*, and who would be one of the three legatees of his poem 'Testament', composed whilst Brett Young was contemplating mortality when lost in M'Kalamo bush in German East Africa during the First World War.

> Three legacies I'll send,
> Three legacies already half possess'd:
> One to a friend, of all good friends the best,
> Better than which is nothing...
> O best of friends, I leave you one sublime
> Summer, one fadeless summer.
> (FDS 24)

Then followed a description of a Cotswold holiday in which the two friends had shared; perhaps the occasion of the composition of the somewhat risqué verses at which other members of the Octette recalled that Brett Young and Hayes were particularly adept. As nothing remotely salacious was ever to appear in Brett Young's published work, this brief insight into student ribaldry paints a very different picture from that of the fastidious English gentleman of later years.

> As I was riding through the Lenches
> I met three strapping country wenches.
> (YP 381)

In examination week, Edwin Ingleby and his friend, Matthew Boyce, decided on a Cotswold holiday to escape from the pressures of student life. Following the identical route taken by Brett Young and Hayes, they composed the identical poem.

> Laughing together, they constructed a series of frankly inde-
> cent couplets, recording the voyager's adventures with all
> three. It was a matter of the most complete collaboration, for
> the friends supplied alternate lines. Edwin provided the final

couplet, which, he declared, gave the composition literary form:
  'Home to my vicarage I hasted
  Feeling the day had not been wasted.'
  (YP 381)

Edwin was Francis and Matthew Boyce, with whom Edwin spent many happy hours in literary rather than medical discussion, was undoubtedly Lionel Hayes, even down to the fine detail that Boyce, like Hayes, was a poet's son.

Like Brett Young, Hayes was to reach the rank of major in the Royal Army Medical Corps, and after seeing service in Europe, would finish his peace-time career as Recruiting Medical Officer for Birmingham. Even though friendship would dissolve in bitterness in later years, a link was maintained, when Hayes' wife Dorothy translated Brett Young novels into Braille. A second member of the Octette who made a career in the army was Edward Selby Phipson, who entered the Indian Medical Service, was mentioned in despatches at Gallipoli, where he was awarded the D.S.O. whilst serving with the Sixth Gurkhas in the advance on Sari Bair heights, and eventually became Inspector-General of Civil Hospitals and Prisons in Assam.

Only two of the Octette were to pursue long-term careers in general practice: Nevill Coghill Penrose and Alfred Ernest Hird, who were both to hold honorary appointments at Birmingham Hospitals which featured in Brett Young novels, Penrose at the General (Brett Young's Infirmary) and Hird at Queen's (Prince's). Both men achieved distinction: Penrose being awarded the O.B.E. in the 1920 New Year's honours for his war-time services at Banbury Auxiliary Hospital and Hird (who remained in Birmingham and became a member of the City Council) being appointed Surgeon Captain in the Naval Volunteer Reserve, after distinguished war service. Nevill Penrose appeared in *The Young Physician* as Denis Martin,

> a tall, loose-limbed creature, with an indefinite humorous face, a close crop of curly fair hair and blue eyes. He seemed approachable, and though his striped flannel suit was more elegant than Edwin's and he wore a school tie of knitted silk, Edwin took the risk of addressing him.
> (YP 235)

It was at Ernie Hird's home in Coventry that Brett Young found respite from study around the time of his medical finals, relaxing with fifty rolls of his orchestral favourites (Brahms, Beethoven, Tchaikovsky and Wagner) played on his friend's pianola.

Brett Young's love of music was also nurtured by his friendship with Bertram Arthur Lloyd, a skilled pianist with a broad musical knowledge, who was eventually to become Professor of Forensic Medicine at the University of Birmingham, where Laurence Ball, the sixth member of the Octette, was appointed Professor of Medicine in the mid-1920s. Brett Young's University of North Bromwich was also the setting for the career of the most distinguished academic of the Octette. Humphrey Francis Humphreys, winner of a Sands Cox scholarship three years after Brett Young, awarded the M.C. for his part in Allenby's Jerusalem campaign, became Professor of Dental Surgery at Birmingham and eventually its Vice Chancellor. In 1936, *Far Forest* was dedicated

For
Humphrey Humphreys
after thirty-three years
of loyal friendship

and when Brett Young died eighteen years later, it was Professor Humphreys who delivered the address at the internment of his ashes in Worcester Cathedral.

The first of the Octette to qualify, Brett Young never attended the periodic reunions celebrated over the next fifty years by this group of intellectual medical students who were all to write, throughout their lives, in a whole range of genres from academic papers to official reports to poetry. However, only Francis turned to writing as a career, abandoning the medical profession for which he was trained and with which all the rest of the Octette remained involved in some measure for the duration of their working lives.

It was at a dance at the Assembly Rooms in the Birmingham suburb of Edgbaston in 1904 that the relationship which was to become the mainstay of Francis Brett Young's life was inaugurated, when Nevill Penrose introduced him to Jessie Hankinson. She was the youngest of the eleven children of John and Margaret Hankinson of Alvechurch in Worcestershire, a farming and hunting family, whose Unitarian forebears originated from Wilmslow in Cheshire, and who were undoubtedly the denominational inspiration, nearly forty years later, for the Isits.

> They came here in the days of the Five Mile Act, which forbade their meeting within that distance of a corporate borough. No doubt they were given a social entree by the fact that they belonged to one of the old North Bromwich Unitarian families, which are our local substitute for an hereditary aristocracy.
> (MAH 4,14-15)

The whole Hankinson family was musical and Jessie destined to become a talented singer, who would perform in Sir Henry Wood's concerts. At this time however, establishing her independence as her free-thinking elder sisters had already done, she had enrolled at Miss Rhoda Anstey's Physical Training College, which, in 1897, had been established at Shenstone's 'Leasowes' in Hales Owen. Fees of one hundred pounds per annum meant that Anstey College was designed for girls who would have an independent life of their own without relying on marriage to support them. Here, in addition to a vegetarian diet, plenty of fresh air and Tuesday afternoon visits to Birmingham University for anatomy lectures, girls followed a two-year training course in outdoor games, dancing, swimming and gymnastics according to Ling's Swedish System. At a similar period, Edie Martyn (herself a youngest sister)

> had taken her Swedish diploma and now, with a new enthusiasm for remedial gymnastics, had established herself in a hospital
> (MBJ 197)

a career reflecting Jessie's service with the Almeric Paget Massage Corps which, like so many of Miss Anstey's students, she joined at the outbreak of the First World War.

An unofficial courtship began, pursued on the Clent Hills where Bella Small would have her short-lived romantic encounter with Henry Fladburn; in the Grand Hotel, Birmingham, where Edward Willis and Celia Stafford, Susan Pennington and Harry Levison would conduct their assignations; and, for a performance of *The Dream of Gerontius*, in Worcester Cathedral, where Catherine Ombersley encountered Dr Selby, who, inspired by the visit, proposed marriage, recalling 'rich personal memories of the day long since, when he had first perceived the emotional significance of Elgar's *Gerontius'* (TLW 592). Amongst the papers deposited in Birmingham University Library after Francis Brett Young's death, was the bound score of *Gerontius* which he gave to Jessie on the occasion of their Worcester visit in 1905.

No doubt the romantic attractions of courting in Virgil's Grove, laid out by his poet-hero, Shenstone, also appealed to Brett Young. However, during one unchaperoned meeting in the lily wood, Jessie and Francis were observed and reported to Miss Anstey, who informed her friend Margaret Young, with the result that, even though Jessie was still invited to The Laurels for musical soirées, relations between Francis and his stepmother cooled still further.

Hindrances to this burgeoning relationship were not found only in Francis's family; none of Jessie's brothers and sisters liked him. Separation was soon to follow when Jessie accepted a post as physical training instructress at the Quaker School at Sidcot in the Mendips, just as Ruth Morgan would be appointed to 'the school for up-to-date young ladies at Cheltenham, where for more than a year she had held the post of games-mistress' (KL 9). Francis was to exert a vicarious influence at Sidcot by writing papers on such topics as 'The Origin of Folk Song and Dance' for Jessie to read to her pupils. Despite her refusal of Francis's first proposal of marriage in June 1905, which she considered precipitate, and the resistance of both of them to a formal engagement, Dr Thomas Brett Young's view that if the relationship meant anything, engagement was essential, ultimately prevailed and Francis and Jessie became officially engaged in November 1906.

The life of a medical student however, was not entirely passed in socialising, and Brett Young, despite his initial resentment at being a Birmingham medic, worked hard and won a Queen's scholarship. He was among the best two or three students of his cohort of thirty-six medical and dental students, passing all his preliminary examinations without difficulty and gaining a First Class in Forensic Medicine, Toxicology and Public Health. At a similar point in his career, Edwin Ingleby came second out of his year and was offered an appointment as prosector with Dr Moon. Though he declined, on the grounds that it would be a drain on his father's pocket for a further year, his creator accepted a similar appointment and became prosector in anatomy with Queen's Hospital surgeon, Arthur Sanders.

As final year medical students, Edwin Ingleby gained experience in the Lower Sparkdale practice of Dr Altrincham-Harris, whilst Brett Young entered the Aston practice of Dr George Bryce, who occasionally lectured at Summer Schools at Miss Anstey's College. Also in 1906, a group of students, of whom Francis was one, took lodgings in Bath Row, Birmingham, hard by Queen's Hospital, in order to be on hand for the fortnight's midwifery which they would undertake in the Birmingham slums. Edwin Ingleby and Matthew Boyce underwent a similar fortnight in Easy Row, the selfsame thoroughfare, where Prince's Hospital was located. The two confinements which Edwin attended were reflections of a case for which Brett Young was responsible.

> In the middle of dinner we were called out to the most filthy, sordid house I have ever entered. A young girl of twenty — her husband out of work ever since their marriage — no help, no light, nothing. Then the mother of the girl came up — hopelessly unintelligent and inclined to be cheeky.
> (FBY 224)

Looking back upon this period, Brett Young was to admit that the long-term benefits compensated for the disappointment which never entirely left him.

> It was my natural destiny as the son and grandson of medical men to earn my living as a doctor. At that time (for I still obstinately thought of myself as a writer) I was foolish enough to resent this arbitrary career. Now I realise that all I know about human nature springs directly from those years spent as a student in the wards of Birmingham hospitals.
> (SHN — GH 05.1935)

From the Birmingham hospital experience came the affectionate lionizing of surgeon Jordan Lloyd, under whose tutelage Brett Young had learned his craft, and who subsequently appeared in three novels as Lloyd Moore,

> that brilliant, wayward genius, the Don Quixote of Midland surgery. Lloyd Moore had become a legend. The presence of the surgeon's frail, boyish figure, its red beard framing a face whose pallor resembled that of an agonised Christ, was an inspiration in itself.
> (MBJ 70)

Only when Jonathan Dakers became Lloyd Moore's house surgeon did he fully appreciate the splendours and responsibilities of his calling. Edwin Ingleby was appointed dresser to Lloyd Moore and soon realised what a privilege it was to work for this outstanding surgical genius, in whose skills he recognised the highest attainment of which surgery was capable. In Dr Bradley's time, the old professor of anatomy was still remembered with respect by the younger medics. Lest the messianic qualities which Brett Young attributed to Jordan Lloyd be considered excessive, they are confirmed by H.W. Pooler, who studied at Queen's Hospital with the same surgeon in an earlier generation. Comparing the real Jordan Lloyd with Brett Young's Lloyd Moore, in *My Life in General Practice*, Pooler commented that not one word of it was untrue or even over-coloured.

Whilst preparing for his final medical examinations in 1905-06, Francis lodged with Gertrude Dale, the daughter of Dr R.W. Dale, the influential social reformer and minister of Carrs Lane Congregational Church in Birmingham. Miss Dale's Edgbaston home was a haven of music and literature and a meeting place for students, in whose lives, activities and friendships she took great interest. Such was the influence of Gertrude Dale that Francis was occasionally persuaded to attend Carrs Lane Church with her in order to hear its famous minister, John Henry Jowett, preach.

John Bradley, in experiencing a variety of life such as he had not known before, visited the Alvaston home of his friend Martin Lacey and found

> its walls hung with pre-Raphaelite drawings and pictures; a library which William Morris had furnished with tapestry hangings and curtains printed in madder and indigo; a painting by Rossetti.
> (DBR 162)

From his student days in Birmingham, Francis never forgot his visit to the house of

> one Holliday, a fossil who has lain hidden in the pre-Raphaelite strata for many years. Oh his Morris! and oh his Rossettis! and oh his Burne Jones! Some of the most gorgeous studies I have ever seen.
> (FBY 252)

Amongst the pre-Raphaelite collection of solicitor James Richardson

Holliday (a near neighbour of Gertrude Dale) over which Brett Young enthused, were Morris's *Minstrel Figure with Shaum*, *Minstrel Figure with Cymbals* and study for *Tristram and Iseult*; Rossetti's *Mephistopheles*, *Sir Galahad at the Ruined Chapel* and *Dante Meeting Beatrice*; and Burne Jones' *The Annunciation*, *The Rape of Proserpine* and *The Tiburtine Sibyl*, all of which Holliday presented to Birmingham Art Gallery in 1927.

Like Edwin Ingleby, who encountered some problems with his finals in the viva-voce examination on surgery, during his finals Brett Young was ill and under considerable strain and felt that he owed his success to the understanding of the examiner in surgery, George Heaton, rather than to his own performance. However, with the receipt of Medical Registration Certificate 4230, his student days came to an end and Francis Brett Young qualified as a doctor.

Though the practice of medicine was destined to occupy only a comparatively short period of Brett Young's life, its ethos would permeate his writing. Many of his characters were doctors: not only eponymous heroes like Bradley and Dakers, but middle order characters like Selby and Weir, as well as minor medics such as Altrincham-Harris, Dench, Hammond, Haskard, Hendry, Martock, Medhurst, Monaghan, Weldon and Wills, who appeared as frequently in non-medical as in medical novels, played their parts and faded from the scene.

Brett Young's doctors surveyed humanity with the heightened perception of medical training not available to laymen. From his limited experience walking the wards of Prince's Hospital, John Bradley 'recognized Laura Munslow as a typical case of chlorotic anaemia which was the most common complaint among the city's young women' (DBR 127-128). Though acquainted with the Captain of the *Chusan* for less time than the rest of its officers, the ship's doctor apprehended signs hidden from them.

> My medical eyes saw more than the fragility of age. The waxen pallor of Shellis's fine face was pathological. I had noticed a sinister pulsation of the carotid denoting aortic incompetence, and suggesting that the old man's hold on life was more precarious than the others realised.
> (CB 8)

The regular sprinkling of medical terminology throughout the stories (auricular fibrillation, bacillary dysentery, Locomotor

Ataxia, phthisis, puerperal septicaemia, transient diplopia) made clear that some awareness of the technical vocabulary of his calling was assumed in Brett Young's readership, who were expected to take in their stride such medical symptoms as those of a North Bromwich tailoress.

> She had stabbed her left forefinger with an infected needle and lit a focus of suppuration in the tendon sheath. Poison was tracking up the lymphatics towards the glands of the axilla that stood like blockhouses in the way of bacterial invasion.
> (YP 344-345)

Indeed, awareness of the effects of the very diseases to which they themselves were prone might well have reached Francis's readers through his writings.

> He had noticed that the stroke was left-sided: which meant that, even if poor George Munslow got over it, he would have lost his speech.
> (DBR 212)

Medical terminology was also employed as appropriate imagery in other areas, as in the increasing stranglehold of Birmingham upon its outlying suburbs.

> The Iron City had developed the encroaching activity of a cancer cell, thrusting greedy tentacles of brick and mortar and steel and cement into healthy countryside: a red and rodent ulcer eating its way into soft green tissue.
> (MMP 179)

Medicine may not have been his first choice of career (or, indeed, his choice at all) but it was to provide the principal storehouse of character, illustration and example from which Francis Brett Young would draw for the rest of his life.

Recognising that his student was exhausted after his medical finals, Dr Heaton suggested the benefits of a spell of sea air. Brett Young had previously toyed with the idea of joining the Royal Navy for a four-year term as ship's doctor, partly to escape the unhappy atmosphere at The Laurels, but it was, in fact, to be the Merchant Navy which claimed his service. Again Edwin Ingleby was used to introduce the next chapter of the adventure.

'What are you going to do?'
'I don't know. A voyage I should think.'
Edwin called for a time-table and looked out the trains to
Liverpool. There was one that started in half an hour. He
caught it, and next morning presented himself at a shipping
office in Water Street.
(YP 468)

In reality, the India Building in Water Street, Liverpool, was home
to the offices of the Blue Funnel Line, the China Mutual Steam
Navigation Co. Ltd and Alfred Holt & Co. Ship Owners, to whom
Francis Brett Young presented himself for interview with one of the
directors, Lt Col Nicholson, in November 1906. Both Francis in fact
and Edwin in fiction were successful in their applications, joining
the ranks of 'boys, recently qualified, taking a last fling at adventure
before settling down' (CHo 211).

Edwin was appointed ship's surgeon aboard the *Macao* at a salary
of £10 a month and bonus, sailing from Birkenhead to China and
calling at Japan for coal en route. Francis was given the identical
posting on the *SS Kintuck*, a steel screw steamer of 4,616 tons, built
for the China Mutual Steam Navigation Co. in 1895 by Workman
Clark & Co. of Belfast and taken over by Alfred Holt's Blue Funnel
Line in 1902. 'The Kintuck is a lovable creature with a funnel of blue
bag blue. My cabin is small but quite delightful, right under the
bridge with a covered gallery open to the sea outside it' (FBY 312).

At the beginning of his adventure, Francis had spent an inaus-
picious

> night in a fifth-rate hotel frequented by sailors, where icy-
> eyed Scandinavians sat stolidly drinking straight whisky. I
> lay in damp sheets on a mattress that was not beyond suspi-
> cion, listening to the wind and the lashing rain.
> (FBY 49)

For Voyage 22 under its master, Captain B.C. Lewis (whom his
new surgeon considered to be modern, genial, gracious, dignified
and polite), the *Kintuck* was to leave Birkenhead at 1.45 p.m. on 5
January 1907, Shanghai and Yokohama being among its ports of call.
On board, in addition to the Chinese crew, were twelve officers,
horrid, dull people, according to Brett Young who was listed as
number eleven. Rather less well paid than Edwin Ingleby, he

received only £8 per month, the equivalent rate to that of the Third Mate, indicative of the unique role of the ship's surgeon.

> The doctor holds a peculiar position in a ship's company. Among these professionals he is counted an amateur; though one of the crew he is never exactly a sailor; though subject to the master's discipline, he is, in his own undisputed province, a specialist. He belongs, in short, to an alien, a shore-side world.
> (CB 15)

The experiences of the *Kintuck* voyage were to provide Brett Young with the framework for a novel, *Sea Horses*, and a whole series of short stories narrated by an unnamed ship's surgeon. The *SS Vega*, the locus of the action of *Sea Horses*, had actually been built for the China tea trade by the old White Funnel Line, however its master, Captain Glanvil, had a friend, who was third officer on a ship of the Blue Funnel line; thus Brett Young's ex-employers found a mention.

The *SS Chusan*, 'a dirty little tramp of two thousand tons' burthen, incredibly grimed and shabby — more like a derelict collier than a live merchantman' (CB 8,2) bound for Japan and China when first she appeared in 'Shellis's Reef', may not have measured up to the description of the *Kintuck*, but she was owned by the Cathay Steam Navigation Company, a very small step in fiction from the China Mutual of fact. The bulk of the *Chusan's* Chinese crew were to be picked up in Hong Kong, though the voyage, described by the ship's surgeon narrator as 'the adventure which I'd been promising myself ever since I graduated: a coloured compensation for six drab years of study...' (CB 1) actually began at Birkenhead. Here, among the half-dozen officers who came on board, was Chief Engineer Twiss, the very name recorded in the *Kintuck's* wages book as that of the Engineer with whom Brett Young sailed. This link with reality was continued in *Sea Horses* where Captain Glanvil's steward, Ah Qui, bore the same name as Brett Young's steward on the *Kintuck*, and the First Mate of both ships, Wallace on the *Kintuck* and Hendry on the *Vega* were Scots. The *Chusan's* surgeon, like his creator was paid £8 per month and suffered from seasickness which was not cured until the downs of Portugal were past. Brett Young was seasick from the first day of his voyage until reaching the Bay of Biscay.

Though captivated by the Portuguese coast, Francis found Cape St Vincent, which he had previously known only from 'Home-Thoughts from the Sea', a disappointment. Looking upon this most unassuming headland, Francis certainly considered himself misled by the effusive description of Browning. It was perhaps not surprising then, that when Edwin Ingleby discussed poets with Matthew Boyce, the fellow-student on whose literary judgement he set such store, 'they spoke of Browning, whose claims to poetry Boyce would not allow' (YP 307). In a similar vein, when trying to dissuade Jim Redlake from literary ambitions, his teacher, Mr Malthus, was equally scathing. '"What modern poets do you admire? Browning? He's still in fashion? No"' (JR 196).

The *Kintuck's* first port of call was Port Said, twelve days into the voyage. The route taken was that which the *Chusan* would take on her voyage to Yokohama, allowing the ships' surgeons of both fact and fiction their first views of 'Gibraltar, grey and monstrous against the dawn; the snows of Crete, flamingo-hued in the fire of sunset; Port Said, where the first smell of the east begins' (CB 14). In Ceylon, the *Kintuck* was invaded by hawkers selling cheap jewellery in much the same way that the *Vega* was boarded by ruffians selling corals in Naples. By the time Penang was reached, the intended remedies of the voyage were beginning to take effect and Brett Young reported gleefully that he had gained eight pounds and never felt fitter. At this unforgettable spot, which Francis visited in a rickshaw with a representative of Holt's local agents, Captain Shellis took his surgeon ashore for a rickshaw tour.

> The memory of that excursion stays with me vividly: the soft, palm-shadowed road; the suburban homes of wealthy Chinese; a flat field, scattered with cloths newly dyed with indigo spread out to dry; and, permeating all, the hot and spicy air of the Malay Peninsula.
> (CB 17)

Hong Kong, Shanghai, Chemulpho and Yokohama, destinations of the *Kintuck* were also destinations of the *Chusan*. When the Chinese New Year of the Sheep (4,604) dawned on 13 February 1907, the *Kintuck* was in the South China Sea, just about to dock at Hong Kong.

> All is bustle fore and aft. The whole Chinese population of the ship are agog, waiting for their new year. At the critical moment they will discharge fizzling fireworks.
> (FBY 317)

The festivities, which lasted up to a fortnight, would have continued as the ship sailed on to Shanghai. Though having no bearing upon the plot of the story, the celebrations in which a Chinese crew engaged on such an occasion, also took place upon the *Chusan*.

> We left Shanghai on the day of the Chinese New Year. I remember it well, for our Chinese crew took the opportunity of going mad. That evening the fo'c's'le grew noisy with the detonations of crackers and fireworks. A smell of burning joss-stick pervaded the ship.
> (CB 21)

When the SS *Chusan* reappeared in *Cotswold Honey*, in a series of short stories, still narrated by its surgeon, though now in East African waters, the plot in each case hinged upon this ocean-going tramp which, like the *Vega* was then described as having been built for the China tea trade, carrying passengers. This too was the basis of the plot of *Sea Horses*. Captain Glanvil, though not averse to carrying a 'cargo' of coolies, pilgrims or emigrants on the well-deck, was unhappy with orders he received from the *Vega's* owners in Liverpool, which result in him carrying passengers. When the *Kintuck* called at Amoy on 23 March 1907, it was to embark a 'cargo' of opium-smoking coolies, who would therefore give little trouble, and for whose health and well-being Dr Brett Young would be responsible. His opinion of the new passengers was, however, somewhat less amenable in a later essay, 'With Chinese Coolies'.

> Some sixty thousand Chinamen leave Amoy every year for the great labour centres of the world. Throughout the Spring months great hordes of active Chinamen are shipped aboard traders, mostly British, for every corner of the globe. We, of the SS *Tuck-kin*, were not overpleased with the prospect of carrying a shipload of celestials from Amoy to Singapore. It meant locked doors and ports and ever-watchful eyes and no small trouble for all concerned.
> (FBY 112)

The normal cargo of the Blue Funnel ships on the China run was cotton and woollen goods on the outward journey, with tea, tin and tobacco on the return, with minimal provision made for the carrying of passengers. On her outward journey, the *Kintuck* was loaded down to the Plimsoll line with road rails destined for Korea, whilst in addition to Chinese passengers, hundreds of tons of sugar made up the cargo for the return journey.

During these months on board ship, Francis did not neglect his literary aspirations. On the outward journey, the splendour of the Indian Ocean provided the setting for his translations of the nineteenth century French poets, Verlaine and de Banville into English verse. By the time of the return journey, he was trying his hand at prose: a humorous story about a dog named McGregor, no doubt inspired by the *Kintuck's* own canine passenger, and a short story in three chapters embracing both the land of his fathers and the opium-smokers of the China seas. 'I am writing a preface to an immortal work and — oh my word — a bloody one. It's called "Roman's Folly"; the scene is laid about Mendip and the gloom of it is fearful beyond words' (FBY 327).

As the voyage progressed towards its conclusion, Francis's thoughts turned to home and to the new life which awaited him there. Above all, home meant Jessie and marriage.

> We are supposed to be in a hurry, and are going home at fourteen knots. Every turn of the screw brings me appreciably nearer to you, and I am almost afraid to think of the happiness which will be ours.
> (FBY 325)

Twenty years later he endowed Jim Redlake with the very thoughts which had passed through his own mind on board the *Kintuck*.

> He would marry Catherine, and the sooner the better. (How languidly the screw churned through the South Atlantic — through the thin-sailed fleets of nautilus and scudding flying-fish!)
> (JR 768)

After a round trip of 125 days, Captain Lewis safely brought the *Kintuck* back to London at 9.45 a.m. on 9 May 1907, where Francis left the ship before it sailed on via Glasgow to Liverpool. Though never to repeat his time as a ship's surgeon, as a result of this voyage, Brett Young had accumulated a series of experiences which would reappear in his writing throughout his career, as his own maritime encounters provided either framework or illustration for his stories.

Four: Borderlands

Shortly after returning from his term of duty on board the *Kintuck*, Francis Brett Young enjoyed the first of a series of walking holidays which were to be particularly significant in his literary development and as a result of which he advanced, and repeatedly emphasized, his claim for serious consideration as a borderlands' writer. His companion on this occasion was the 'gentle poet and stern critic' to whom *Robert Bridges: A Critical Study* was later dedicated. Alfred Hayes (1857-1936), minor poet, dramatist and translator, keen botanist and musician, was the father of Lionel Hayes of the Octette. Their destination was the England-Wales border, in fact the environs of Llanthony Abbey, that narrow promontory of Monmouthshire thrust between Breconshire and Herefordshire, where the irascible Walter Savage Landor briefly made his home.

Ramblers in Brett Young's novels also visited Llandewi, actually the ruins of the Augustinian Priory of St John the Baptist at Llanthony, a place of startling beauty, which his description did not understate.

> In the midst of a basin of pale green — like some singular work of art for which a collector has chosen the perfect setting — a group of stone masonry, which included a massive tower and the Gothic arches of a ruined nave, took their breath with sudden surprise and wonder that left them speechless.
> (MLF 226)

Further explorations in Grwyne Fawr alerted Francis to the lonely wildness of Urishay Castle, which he renamed Trecastel,

> one of the great castles built upon the Brecon March to keep an eye upon the border Welsh. I suppose that March is about the most romantic patch of countryside in England.
> (DT 56)

Such then was the locale from which Francis wrote to Jessie describing the peace of the great black mountains, which had filled his heart with longing. This wistfulness first gave focus to the Arcadia which would emerge, through a whole series of novels, as a spiritual homeland: a retreat to which both Brett Young and his characters would regularly make their escape from the trivial round and common task.

> In the summer of 1911, I had brooded and walked much about the upper waters of the Teme — perhaps with a great deal of *A Shropshire Lad* in mind, and not unnaturally, for A.E. Housman, born, as I was, under the shadow of the Clents, had found a westward escape by the same paths.
> (BD Preface viii)

'Escape' appropriately described the journeys of Brett Young characters such as Susan and Dick Pennington and Owen Lucton, who followed that same westward route.

Faced by the responsibilities of married life, for which they were ill-prepared, increasing debt, the imminent prospect of both unemployment and parenthood, allied with the need to escape the burdens of life in a demanding North Bromwich suburb, it was at Chapel Green on the Radnorshire border that Mr and Mrs Pennington sought refuge.

> As they crossed Severn above Bewdley, Dick underwent an odd metamorphosis. It was as though the passage of that boundary washed away from his mind all the heavy preoccupations of the last months. The reason why he expanded and bloomed in this new land west of Severn was that his spiritual roots reached far and deep into ancestral soil.
> (MMP 307-8)

The same metamorphosis claimed Susan Pennington, though her vision had never before extended so far.

> The valley of Teme, as Dick remembered it now, shone through his lame words with a tender, mystical radiance. As he spoke, he seemed to Susan to make life sound so sweet and sane, so much nearer to its holy source than it had ever appeared before.
> (MMP 104)

In this borderland, both Penningtons enjoyed an idyllic interlude of supreme contentment, in which even the would-be sophisticate, Susan, an average product of industrial suburban life, confessed that never before had she been so happy. The return to the Midlands inevitably brought tragedy, the final glimmer of future hope being found only in exile to Ludlow, where their story ended.

Dismayed and disillusioned by the mundane routine of a prosperous but unfulfilling life of business, Owen Lucton set out for a drive in his new eight cylinder Pearce-Tregaron, one of the symbols of his success. Taking the road from Halesby into Worcestershire, Bredon Hill was the object of his conscious choice, even though the borderlands drew him, as to some compulsive Eden.

> Beyond Halesby rose the undulant line of the Clents, last outpost of the mountainous west. Mr Lucton knew well what wonders were visible from those twin summits: not merely the Clees and the Wrekin, but all the hills beyond Severn — Woodbury, Abberley, Ankerdine, the Malverns, and, westward again, the mountains of Wales. It was odd, he reflected, how, all through his life, that prospect had drawn his imagination westward, as though it had expected to find there some lost paradise.
> (MLF 65)

Involved in a motor accident on the road to Pershore, Mr Lucton seized the moment which had never come before and might never again return. Leaving Bredon behind, he headed for Malvern, gladly surrendering himself to the call of the inevitable.

> The green foothills of the Malverns rolling away into Herefordshire, and beyond them all the tumbled hills of the Marches of Gwent and Radnor. 'The March of Wales,' Mr Lucton thought. The phrase was an incantation. Repeating the words for the mere relish of their sound, he was exalted and drunk with them. 'The March of Wales ... Of course, that's where I'm going.'
> (MLF 167,170)

Progressing via Llandewi, Felindre and Chapel Green, Mr Lucton also found his promised land, the 'quietest under the sun', around the upper waters of the Teme, where, like his creator, he too had *A Shropshire Lad* much in mind. Here his spirits would be restored and his strength renewed, and he would discover the necessary resource to return to the daily routine of North Bromwich, the promise for the future being that life would never be quite the same again.

However, not all who sought spiritual or economic renewal in the Welsh Marches and the borderlands were to find it there. Out of work (the revenge of a gerrymandering employer upon his refusal to throw a football cup-tie), in danger of becoming too friendly with his young stepmother and quite unable to co-exist peaceably with his drunken father, Abner Fellows determined to cut himself free from the snares of life in Halesby and make a fresh start in pastures new. Well-paid work was always to be found in Coventry and the distance was short for one who had no money to spare for travel. But Coventry did not offer the new life that Abner sought. As the sun rose one morning, he made his way to the top of Uffdown, where the cool, clean air cleared his brain and aided his decision.

> He wanted to make a clean start in a new country. As the mists ascended, showing May Hill and Malvern, Abberley, Clee and all the nearer hills of Wales, he knew that they promised freedom. He decided on Wales.
> (BD 114)

The downward spiral of the remainder of Abner's adventures and the bulk of the story of *The Black Diamond* was played out in the borderlands around the Garon pipeline: in Lesswardine, Chapel Green, Wolfpits, Llandwlas, Redlake and Brampton Bryan, bringing him finally to Shrewsbury and the King's Shilling, without ever having found the freedom that he had so earnestly desired.

Brett Young's walking tour of the Welsh Marches of summer, 1911 was planned as a respite from medical practice and in order to avoid being caught up in the musical festivities at Brixham with which the coronation of King George V and Queen Mary would be celebrated. Beginning at Ludlow and walking the hilltops where, under Francis's direction Jessie did not escape from practising her scales, these wayfarers also visited places such as Brampton Bryan, Bucknall and Leintwardine, where the more established author of later years would enjoy his usual springtime relaxation: fishing for grayling and trout on the River Teme.

Further holidays at Llanthony were spent with Francis's brother, Eric, the co-author of both *Robert Bridges* and *Undergrowth*, a story of turbulent mysticism, which ultimately sold one thousand copies.

(Eric's early journalistic training, which eventually led to a career with *Hansard* and the writing of two detective stories, *The Murder at Fleet* and *The Dancing Beggars*, was partly financed by Francis, who paid the premium required for Eric's apprenticeship with a Liskeard weekly newspaper.) It was during visits to the Welsh borderlands that the plan for the critical study of Bridges took shape, and the setting for *Undergrowth*, the partly excavated but subsequently abandoned reservoir in the Grwyne Valley, first explored.

The ambitious scheme which permanently united Birmingham with Radnorshire and redefined the borderlands in between, was one of the great engineering feats of Brett Young's boyhood. An Act of Parliament of July 1892 allowed Birmingham Corporation to dam the rivers Elan and Claerwen, pipe water to the city by aqueduct and construct the railway required to transport the necessary building materials. This municipal concupiscence was captured in an early commentary on the second city's appetite.

> Its tentacles spread into the wet and lonely valley of the Garon, from where the council had decreed, the rain of the water-shed, which geology had destined for the Wye and later for the Atlantic, must now traverse eighty miles of conquered territory, and after being defouled by the domestic usages of North Bromwich, must find its way into the Trent, and so to the North Sea.
>
> (YP 227)

James Mansergh was the engineer responsible for Craig Goch, Pen-y-Garreg and Caban Goch dams, which were opened by King Edward VII in July 1904. By 1905, the whole of Birmingham was supplied with water via the pipeline which ran from Rhayader to Frankley Reservoir. Cycle rides in exploration of this embryonic pipeline captured Brett Young's adolescent imagination and provided a subject which would both inspire and endure.

> Searching for some common factor, I hit upon the theme of the Welsh water-supply. The pipe-line traversed all that country which was the cradle of my young imagination. My father's surgery at Hales Owen was daily crowded with navvies, whose corduroys were stained with the red earth of the workings. Here was the unifying factor I wanted. My Midland novels were to be strung along that pipe-line as beads are threaded on a string.
>
> (BD Preface vii-viii)

In a succession of stories, representing all stages of his career, Brett Young painted a series of graphic pictures, some occupying entire novels, others no more than brief cameos, illustrating the enormity of the challenge of the Welsh water scheme; sinister machinery and interminable labour in combat with the awesome powers of Nature. Human ingenuity would eventually prevail and the earth, red as the blood observed by the doctor's eye, would ultimately be subdued, but not before death had ravaged the borderlands.

The building of the dams, which dominated *Undergrowth* and *The House Under The Water*, also featured in other Mercian novels. Mansergh, in Brett Young's canon, became Barradale, though it was his young assistant Charles Lingen, who had the first vision, the seeds of which were not explained until the final novel.

> Charles was dreaming of mountain streams impounded in man-made lakes, whose contents would flow on to slake the thirst of cities hundreds of miles away from the lonely uplands on which they were tamed.
> (W 135)

More than forty years before these words were published, *Undergrowth*, the story in which Nature, in spirit and in power, fought back against man's attempts to harness her forces, pictured the building of a dam in the Black Mountains where

> the river waters were soon to be imprisoned. Gangs of workmen, in clothes stained with the colour of the soil, swarmed in trenches. Above them the razor-edge of the dam, a wall of blackish sandstone, bridged the valley head. On its top the beam of a crane swung swiftly, black against a cloud of escaping steam.
> (U 9)

Gunner Eve, the one-eyed foreman who directed the gang building the dam in *Undergrowth*, exerted a similar authority in *The Young Physician* where the laying of the pipe-line was a task just as intractable.

> Edwin heard a sound of spades and pick-axes and came upon a group of navvies working at a cutting of red earth that was already deep on either side of the road. It seemed to him a noble sight. 'What are you working at?' he asked. 'Is it a railway?'

'To hell with your railway,' said the Gunner. 'It's a pipe-track. This here's the Welsh water scheme. And a black job it is, I can tell you.'
(YP 145-146)

By the time Abner Fellows sought casual work with the Welsh water scheme, Gunner Eve, by then engaged in relaying a defective section of pipe beyond Chapel Green, two miles from Lesswardine, was just one of the workers for whom the pipeline was the whole of their world.

The clerk of the works had been as long on the waterworks job as Gunner Eve himself. Year after year he had led a nomadic life, moving from one point to another of the great pipe-line. The piece of work on which Abner was engaged was the result of one of the last feeble struggles of the gods of stone against their iron masters. The pipe-line had been lodged upon a deposit of old red sandstone; a hidden leak had distorted its bedding.
(BD 179)

Maintenance still continued at the time when Susan Pennington stayed with Aunt Judith at Chapel Green, where a group of workmen in corduroys were employed on the waterworks scheme. Susan was warned that '"they'm blasting a double track for the North Bromwich pipe-line. You have to keep your eyes skinned on this road when they fire their charges"' (MMP 312). Unfortunately, Susan failed to heed the advice and the subsequent explosion prefaced her tragedy.

It was in *The House Under The Water* that the plot first rehearsed thirty years earlier in *Undergrowth*, was powerfully and convincingly developed. In this epic tale, a solitary mansion house near Pont Escob was doomed by the building of the reservoir which flooded its valley. Though the story is fictional, two mansions (Cwm Elan and Nant Gwyllt, where Shelley took his Harriet) were actually submerged when the valleys of Elan and Claerwen were flooded to create the reservoirs from which Birmingham's water supply was drawn. Construction work again began with the violence and devastation previously witnessed in *Undergrowth*.

Across the valley stretched a furrow dug down to the rock, like a military entrenchment, beside which the shunting

engines deposited a whole armament of gigantic excavating machinery: vertical rock-drills driven by steam from hissing boilers; pile-drivers that looked like guillotines; travelling cranes that dipped and raised their arms like the trunks of elephants; great navvy-devils, whose sharp-lipped buckets scraped into the debris and lifted it, a ton at a time.
(HUW 537)

However, this story progressed, succeeding where *Undergrowth* failed; though Nature again retaliated, human invention and technological skill triumphed and the scream of machinery was followed by a profound silence, heralding a devastation still more profound.

A silence not only deathlike but deadly. The flood rose and rose, seeping downwards into every cranny that sheltered life, till those that were little and could not fend for themselves were drowned where they cowered, and those that could escape slunk away or sat paralysed by fear, till the rising death lapped their feet and drove them before it, dazed and helpless.
(HUW 551-552)

Though the valley had to die for the life and sanitation of the remotely indifferent citizens of North Bromwich, time would bring its own resurrection, even where death had been most violent.

Cloud vanished from the sky, but no blue shone back from the water. It needed time before the suspended matter, sinking downward, settling ceaselessly, spread its coating on the motionless branches and leaves of drowned trees, on rocks and on hedgerows, covering all with the hues of death, until the water's surface grew crystal-clear, flawed by wavelets that danced in the sun with a brisk, glistening gaiety.
(HUW 556)

A generation later, the route which Mr Lucton followed from North Bromwich into the borderlands, took him well south of the pipeline. Nevertheless, as a reader of popular fiction, Forest Fawr in Radnorshire was familiar to him.

'That's where the North Bromwich water comes from. There's a house — a house under the water. I've always wanted to see it.'
'I suppose you've read that book. Well you can't see much

of it now: just a bit of garden wall when the lake runs low.'
(MLF 276-277)

Repeated holidays in the 1920s would take the Brett Youngs, with friends from the Octette, to a bungalow belonging to the Birmingham Corporation at Pen-y-Garreg in the Elan Valley. Here Francis would absorb the atmosphere and fish the lakes, born out of the destruction so vividly portrayed in his writing. It was during one such holiday that Francis and Jessie, Humphrey Humphreys and Leo Hayes returned to the cottage after a Saturday hike, to find an unlit fire, no hot water, and the cook on her knees in fervent prayer, her Seventh Day Adventist principles offended by this flagrant misuse of the Day of the Lord. A decade later, this very character was recreated in Thirza Moule.

> 'The Day of the Lord will show. It's coming much sooner than you think. On the Seventh Day. Let us pray.'
> And there, on the grimy floor of the chain-house, without further warning, she knelt. She prayed aloud, in a high whining voice, about the fire and chariots and the whirlwind and the Wrath of the Lamb. It seemed, indeed, as though Mrs Moule might go on praying indefinitely, until, all of a sudden, she said 'Amen,' rose from her knees, and, brushing the grit from her skirt, became normal and business-like.
> (FF 32-33)

So it was that the borderlands west of Severn were to become for Francis Brett Young the place both of regeneration and of inspiration. If the setting of a novel were not actually to be located there, geography could yet give birth to idea. It was during the vacation of 1911, on passing the vicarage at Leintwardine, that Francis first spoke of his intention of writing, one day, a book about a girl who lived there, who would have red hair and be called Celia Stafford. Sure enough, five years later, *The Iron Age* contained a chapter entitled 'Lesswardine' and a character named Celia Malpas, with thick chestnut hair, who left her brother behind at the parsonage at Aston-by-Lesswardine on moving to the industrial Midlands with her new husband, Charles Stafford.

Further fascination with the borderlands was expressed in recollections of Captain Robert Dolbey, a surgeon with whom Brett Young served in East Africa and to whom *for love of Temeside*, he dedicated *Sea Horses*. 'I love him much for himself and possibly more (that is the way I am made) because his home is near the Long Mynd in Shropshire' (FBY 480). The appreciation which Brett Young wrote in *The Times* when Dolbey died of appendicitis in 1937, drew attention to his Marcher origins and that he would be laid to rest among his border ancestors in Wistanstow Churchyard, facing Wenlock Edge.

The ambience of the borderland landscape was a continually recurring presence; its people, its customs and its history appeared at all points of the spectrum, extending its domains into Worcestershire, almost as far as Brett Young's own birthplace, and certainly beyond that which would normally be considered the lands of the Marcher Lords. Sometimes the infusion of the borderlands was the linchpin without which the whole plot failed, as in the short story, 'Mr Walcot Comes Home' or the full-length novel, *Jim Redlake*.

Descended as he was from one of the great Marcher families, the Mortimers, Jim Redlake's migration to the borderlands was nothing less than a retracing of his own roots and a working out of his own salvation, in which the attentive reader will discover elements of Brett Young's own pilgrimage. Jim's journey began at the nuclear family home at Sedgebury in the Black Country and proceeded to the adoptive household of his maternal grandparents at Thorpe Folville in High Leicestershire. From here Jim progressed, via school at Winchester, to university at London, where (in response to the debt which he believed he owed to his doctor-grandfather) he began the medical training which he would soon abandon for the writing which had always been his ambition. By way of the German East African Tanga Campaign, where he contracted malaria whilst serving under General Smuts, Jim eventually entered upon the inheritance for which the whole of his life had both prepared and fitted him: the Trewern estates, near Lesswardine.

> It was from those remote hills of the Radnor March, near a village called Lesswardine, that his mother's ancestors had sprung. He soon spotted Lesswardine on a ragged Bartholomew reduction of the Ordnance Survey; but try as he would, he could not remember what his mother's ancestral home was called, till suddenly its name, staring him in the face, brought everything back to him. Trewern, that black dot on the mountainous brown of Clun Forest, represented the ultimate bourne of his backward pilgrimage.
>
> (JR 419, 423)

Sometimes there was merely a passing reference, such as investing Lady Helena Pomfret's fiancé, Viscount Ledwyche, with a border title in the short story 'Eros and Psyche'. Sometimes it was from the towns and villages of the borders that Brett Young's characters received their baptism. The eponymous heroes, Owen Lucton, Jim Redlake and Ludlow Walcot; major characters such as Alaric Grosmont and Jane Weston; minor ones like Mary Condover and Morgan Malpas; whole dynasties of the Clun and Pomfret families spread throughout several novels all took their names from the borderlands. Sometimes the Marches were a remembered background, left behind, but never entirely forgotten.

By its fifteenth page, the setting of *The Crescent Moon* had moved from the borderlands of her roots to German East Africa and into the flashback in which Eva Burwarton emerged from the terrors of a life more awful and yet more thrilling than she ever thought possible. Despite the horrors which had set their mark upon her, her origins had left a yet deeper mark.

> The girl's face brought to me the atmosphere of that sad and beautiful country which lies along the March of Wales. The impression was so distinct that I could have affirmed: 'This woman comes from the Welsh Marches somewhere between Ludlow and Usk.'
> (CM 3-4)

Recalling her homeland helped for a little while to ease the pain of the loss which Eva suffered during the traumatic days of the Waluguru uprising.

> Suddenly her whole face brightened. We pieced together a fairly vivid picture of the scattered group of houses above the forest of Wyre, where the high road from Bewdley climbs to a place called Clows Top. From here you can see Brown Clee and Titterstone in two great waves; and hear on a Sunday evening, the church bells of Mamble and Pensax, villages whose names are music in themselves. People live easy lives in those parts ... the quietest under the sun.
> (CM 8-10)

Employing the closing lines of the traditional rhyme which Housman used in *A Shropshire Lad*, Brett Young created the contrast between what was remembered and what was experienced in *The

Crescent Moon, underlining his conviction that a borderlands origin was a permanently recognisable influence, but not necessarily one which would always live up to the high expectations of those who recalled it.

On the final night of his working life in Wednesford, where personal tragedy had dogged his path, Dr Bradley's thoughts returned to his borderland roots, memories of which had lain dormant in his subconscious for more than half a century. It was, however, vague euphoria rather than concrete recollection which enticed his imagination back to Elysium. The reality was that distance, both of time and space, had lent unwarranted enchantment to a dream and Dr Bradley invested the borderlands of his childhood with the aura of paradise; a paradise which there was no reason to suppose that the carefree enthusiasm of those youthful, halcyon days would not have discovered elsewhere.

> Though he had never set foot in Lesswardine since he left it at the age of nineteen, Dr Bradley had always preserved a private vision of the place. He could not remember the most impressive features in the landscape: what he remembered most was the quietude and sweetness of the air, the general atmosphere of ease and irresponsibility. Such were the sensations to which Dr Bradley's memory clung, those which in retirement he had set his mind on recapturing.
>   (DBR 40-42)

Such was the attraction of the Welsh Marches for Francis Brett Young that it seemed as if his physical as well as his spiritual roots were to be found there. In a review of *The House Under The Water*, the Georgian poet and playwright Gordon Bottomley referred to the ancestral memory which stirred and became incandescent in Brett Young when he wrote of the Welsh Marches. With the same novel in mind, the Archdruid who admitted Brett Young to the bardic title of *Claerwenydd* at the Gorsedd held at Wrexham on 10 August 1933, referred to him as a novelist of the borders. A decade later when the eminent historian G.M. Trevelyan reviewed *The Island* for *The Observer*, he spoke in general of Brett Young's deep interest in the history of England, English countryside and countryfolk, but in particular of his love of Worcestershire and the Welsh borders where his own roots lay.

It was in the foreword to 'Pastoral Symphony: A.D. 1743', one of the sections of *The Island*, that the indissoluble link between Worcester-shire and the Welsh borders was made clear. At the compilation of the Domesday Book, Hales Owen, part of the Clent Hundred, Brett Young's birthplace and the setting for 'Pastoral Symphony', once in the County of Salop, was part of the manor of Roger de Montgomery, one of the Marcher lords who became Earl of Shrewsbury in 1074. Far distant though eighteenth century Hales Owen may have been from the actual borderlands, its resemblance to them was unmistakable.

> Here one might imagine oneself on the borders of Wales; for the landscape is wild and tumbled: a country of combe and coppice, sparsely cultivated, and cloven by deep valleys through which flow numerous brooks. There are many hedged fields of small size and irregular shape, of the kind that characterize Herefordshire and Shropshire today.
> (I 266)

Thus Brett Young laid claim to the ancestral memory to which genealogy did not otherwise entitle him.

Though living then in Halesby, far-removed from her childhood home, the summit of Uffdown, from which Brett Young looked down upon the whole of his little world, allowed Beatrice Ingleby one final view of the indisputable borderland of her fathers, distant Felindre (the very same retreat selected by Dr Henry Malcolm for his 'away from it all' fishing trip in the short story, 'A Busman's Holiday').

> Her forefathers had once been great people, living in a stone border castle high above the Monmouth marches. 'Those hills that look like mountains cut out of blue cardboard are the Malverns, and far, ever so far beyond them a level ridge drops suddenly in the west. It's the mountain close to where I was born. Part of it's in Wales; Felindre's in England.'
> (YP 33-34)

Accurate though the remainder of the detail of the mother-son relationship undoubtedly was in *The Young Physician*, Brett Young's maternal ancestors of course came, not from the Welsh Marches at all, but from Somerby in Leicestershire, which cannot be seen from the top of the Clent hills! The shift in reality at this point, therefore, served both to bring the hero's visible roots within the scope of the author's stated literary compass, and also to underline his enduring affinity with those borderlands which lay at the very limit of his boyhood vision as either spiritual retreat or ancestral home.

Five: Brixham

When Dr Edwin Ingleby returned from his fictional sea voyage, it was to take up the post of house surgeon at Prince's Hospital, North Bromwich: when Dr Francis Brett Young returned from his factual journey to the East, it was to two brief locum-tenancies in the Midlands. In June/July 1907 he deputised in the Hockley surgery of Dr William McCall, an episode which he obviously had no desire to prolong.

> Heaven preserve me from the privilege of possessing such
> a practice as this. I have never had space to breathe since I
> took it on. The work is beyond words killing.
> (FBY 332)

Nevertheless, the following month saw him repeating the experience in Bloxwich with Dr James McDonald, where he was called to attend some of the most terrible cases he ever met in his whole life. The rigours of medicine did not prevent Brett Young from continuing with his literary efforts and it was during his time at Bloxwich that 'Roman's Folly' was finished.

This short Midlands interlude provided the opportunity for Francis to seek out a permanent medical practice. In this he was assisted by Mr Shorthouse of Philip Harris & Co. the Birmingham chemical and medical suppliers. When John Bradley was in a similar position, an 'old firm of wholesale druggists who conducted an agency for the sale of medical practices gave him numerous introductions' (DBR 296). When Francis, no doubt with tongue in cheek, translated Mr Shorthouse into Mr Longmead, the assistance given to Jonathan Dakers was even more clearly defined. 'Mr Longmead, the manager at Edmonsons', succeeded in finding the very thing; a practice at Wednesford, in the heart of the Black Country' (MBJ 93-94). As a result of Shorthouse's advice, Francis settled in Brixham, Devon, where six hundred pounds (the very amount which Dr Bradley would later invest in his Sedgebury practice) bought him a partnership with Dr William Jenkins Quicke of Cleveland House in New Road. The original intention was that the senior partner would retire after three years. However, the ever-critical Brett Young, who was lodging in nearby Cumbers, considered that he was doing all the work for less than half the pay, and did not share the opinion of many of Quicke's established patients with whom the old doctor was popular.

> Quicke is the worry of my life. I don't know how I shall stand three years of him. If he was sane or amenable to reason I should not so much object. But he's unconscionably slow. He is also half mad.
> (FBY 336/349)

The practice did have distinct possibilities for a young man with energy and promised to yield in the region of £650 a year. Quicke, whom Francis soon discovered was addicted to cocaine and showed not the least desire to be rid of the habit, was persuaded to retire early and Brett Young moved into Cleveland House (now the presbytery of the Church of Our Lady Star of the Sea), with its tiny surgery and dining room leading into the walled garden with flowering chestnut, apple, magnolia and fig trees. Upstairs was a music room, with William Morris curtains and the Bechstein piano which Francis had bought in Torquay. At the back of the house, a dark and damp lumber-room provided space for the aspiring author to pursue his writing. With this rather unsatisfactory study Brett Young, who confessed that he needed the sunshine if he was to write, had to be content.

With the practice came Gladys, the black mare who pulled the dog cart in which the new doctor was to visit his patients. Nesta Job became cook-housekeeper, Fred Cole was the groom and a surgery maid completed the modest household.

Francis fell in love with the town from the first: 'Brixham is lovely beyond words. No big hotel, no pier, no pierrots or theatre; just a small beautiful harbour with 250 trawlers with brown sails' (FBY 336). In this seaside town, he was to find leisure to experiment with the fascination which had captivated him since his preparatory school days and which would come to fulfilment with the publication of *The House Under The Water* a quarter of a century later. 'I spent a glorious hour making sand dams in the rock pools, diverting rivers and drowning villages and generally gratifying my engineering whims' (FBY 432).

Within a very short while, the practice was showing signs of growth and in March 1908 an additional surgery was opened in nearby Galmpton, with at least one new patient added to Brett Young's list — 'only a farm labourer so do not crow' (FBY 367). No doubt with memories of his father's style of doing things in Hales Owen, Francis knew that if he wished to increase the private side of the practice, there was one sure way to go about it. 'The patients are getting to know me: but I want the better class and unless I get social and churchy I'm afraid it'll be a job' (FBY 431). Perhaps this accounted for the reason why two roles in which Brett Young made a name for himself in Brixham were as an enthusiastic worker for the local Conservative party and conductor of the local choral society. Whilst some of his patients were not even aware that they harboured an embryo author in their midst, others considered that their new doctor showed a greater interest in literature than in medicine. The truth of the matter is contained in Brett Young's own description of his method of marrying writing with general practice:

> An hour or two a day were shamelessly snatched from the jaws of inexorable duty. In a small upper room, faithfully guarded by my wife from the assaults of the telephone and the surgery bell, I sat writing. As a result *The Dark Tower* was written in just under two months.
> (DT Preface ix)

Just as the people of Brixham were assessing Brett Young, so he observed them, as he followed the football team around the county to its local derbies and soaked up the appropriate topographical atmosphere which would be recalled for Mawne United's match against the Albion Reserves: 'From the crowd a low murmur arose like the noise of the sea breaking on distant shingles; the team emerged; the crowd swayed and the murmur swelled to a roar' (BD 70). His professional duties gave him further insights. 'I've just had a young man in the surgery with a huge bite in his cheek given him by a young woman at a Church Garden Fête. Do not these people enjoy themselves?' (FBY 403) The puritanical standards of church life in Brixham, where unmarried members of the congregation were segregated for their moral wellbeing, were accurately recounted in

Reuben Henshall's experience.

> Even if you are keeping company with a young woman you
> may not sit by her side at St Peter's. The long and narrow floor
> of the church is split by the central passage into two blocks of
> conflicting colour, one of sober navy blue, the other flightily
> diversified.
> (DS 82-83)

House visits were frequently the occasion both for hearing again
the call of Africa, which had first stirred Brett Young's childish
imagination at The Laurels, and for the inclinations of the writer to
obscure those of the doctor.

> Often when I went into the houses of my patients, I used to
> come across curios brought home from African ports: carved
> wooden spoons, stools and idols; rough musical instruments;
> huge fantastic shells. Then for a moment I used to forget the
> pain in Mrs Brokenshire's back and go off into a daydream of
> which any reputable doctor should have been ashamed.
> (FBY 32)

Though Francis was separated from Jessie, who was still teaching
at Sidcot, those early Brixham months saw a flowering of their
relationship, the poetic origins of which stretched back to the time
before their engagement.

> I am sending you a book of poems which are a great favourite
> of mine. Austin Dobson realises in a large degree my ideals
> of the perfect litterateur. He is always refined; but for a few
> suspicions of sentimentality here and there, he is contempla-
> tive and sweet!
> (FBY 173)

This heightened development, which coincided with Francis entering
the third of Shakespeare's seven ages of man, was well documented
by his creative activity, which, at this period, was musical rather than
literary. The schoolboy who had taught himself to play the piano
had evolved into the lover whose emotions would be expressed
through his musical compositions: a few piano pieces and in excess
of thirty songs, some of which, though composed during the year
before his removal to Cleveland House, were first publicly performed

during the Brixham years. Using other men's words to give voice to his own state of mind, Brett Young marked this dawn of a new era in his life by the choice of the poetry which he set to music. The fact that they were other men's words was of far less significance than that they were the words which Brett Young selected out of all those available to him as the leitmotif of his songs.

For his early attempts he turned to the seventeenth century, first to Robert Herrick's' 'To Electra' with its description of the poet's sole desire only to kiss the air which his love had breathed. Both the poem and the setting were to remain among Brett Young's favourites, causing his 'heart always to beat a trifle faster when I sing it — as, indeed, it beat when I wrote it' (FBY 249). Herrick's works were an appropriate preliminary to Suckling's 'Why so pale and wan, fond lover?' which in turn would lead suitably into the nineteenth century and a temporary reinstatement of Browning, whose eulogistic 'Song' praised the tresses of his mistress's hair. However, it was not only poets long dead whom Francis enlisted to speak those words which he was not, as yet, ready to speak for himself.

From the nineteenth century, came verses from minor British writers such as George Whyte-Melville, better known for the sporting and historical novels which made up the library in the Wednesford surgery where Jonathan Dakers had his practice, and W.E. Henley, remembered for his dramatic collaborations with R.L. Stevenson. Brett Young's setting of Charles Kingsley's 'Airly Beacon' aroused the interest of both Granvill Bantock and Edward Elgar. Edgar Allan Poe's 'To Helen' and Longfellow's translation of Froissart's 'Rondell' represented the American tradition. Norman Gale (1862-1942), a rural poet in the tradition of Herrick; the prize-winning poet and dramatist, Stephen Phillips (1864-1915); and Dubliner, W.B. Yeats (1865-1939) all provided Francis with inspiration, as did William Watson (1878-1935), whom he greatly admired. Typical from the writings of these contemporary poets was the lover's vision in Watson's 'The Voice From Dreamland', fading with the coming dawn and leaving the visible earth less real than the memory; or the melancholy of 'April', again by Watson, in which laughter was rapidly transposed to tears. In the light of these choices, it was not surprising that Francis should have admitted that nearly everything he wrote was full of melancholy; nor that sadness should be the keynote of his setting of verses from *In Memoriam*. Further renderings of Tennyson's verse revealed a similar interpretation.

> I have beguiled the hours by setting in a frame of appropriate
> melancholy and simplicity 'Edward Gray'. The last three bars
> of each verse should be almost staccato in their distinctions
> and expressionless in their simplicity. Expressionless? No —
> teeming with passion and pathos but marked with simplicity.
> (FBY 166)

Critics who were later to accuse Brett Young of using ten words
where four would have served him better, may have discovered a
foretaste of this trait in the liberal sprinkling of florid musical
directions included in his settings. As many as a dozen different
instructions per page direct both singer and accompanist: *allargando;
andante misterioso; inflessibilmente; morendo; poco crescendo; teneramente.*
Where the Italian would no longer serve, he resorted to English: *with
breadth; drag it as much as possible — the more the better.*

The verses which were chosen as suitable to become songs, principally for Jessie to sing with Francis as accompanist, certainly
verified Shakespeare's vision of the lover sighing like a furnace and
singing, as his own song, the ballads of others, made, if not actually
to his mistress' eyebrow, then at least to the tresses of her hair or the
space she had lately occupied.

Even when not engaged in setting verse to music, other people's
poetry remained a dominant means of expression for Brett Young's
fervour and declaration of his feelings. Once, on returning to Hales
Owen after a visit to Jessie's Alvechurch home he had

> trudged along with my head full of love and hope and anxi-
> eties — till the steady swing of my walk resolved itself into
> the metre of a poem by Housman, and I mentally repeated it
> a hundred times:
> > White in the moon the long road lies
> > That leads me from my love.
> (FBY 162)

At meetings of the Octette, Brett Young frequently sang his settings of
Watson or Bridges or Housman, his hearers knowing most of *A
Shropshire Lad* by heart.

Once settled in Brixham, Francis continued to explore his talent
for composition, setting poems by both Housman and Shelley
('To-morrow' and 'The Faded Violet') to music. However, it was his
Songs of Robert Bridges, dedicated 'To H.E.G.D.' (Harriet Elizabeth

Gertrude Dale), that was eventually to be published by Breitkopf & Hartel. Brett Young viewed the next Laureate as a poet who had made a religion of love. It was, then, not surprising that the nine poems arranged for voice and pianoforte in *Songs* that were chosen from among Bridges' verses which Francis had set to music, should have focused upon the passion and wistfulness of the lover seen in the earlier arrangements of Herrick, Suckling, Browning and Watson. In the selection from Bridges, the rays of the moon shone only upon the poet and his love; love was that which haunted dreams and seemed so sweet; it was the divine gift which fell on the heart from heaven. As a counterpoise to this came a melancholy suggestive of Victorian emotionalism. The hero of 'Folk Song' mourned for his dead love; in the joyful 'Larks', there was a mournful mist that blotted out the day; even 'The Sea Poppy' knew no lovers like its red counterpart. Occasional subtle changes in the text suggested that the exigencies of medical practice in Brixham had failed to introduce realism at least into this aspect of the young poet's life, and that Dr Francis Brett Young's view of mortality was at variance with that of Dr Robert Bridges. Where Bridges wrote 'when death to either shall come,' Brett Young substituted 'if death to either should come'!

In 1913 Messrs Weeks & Co. published *Songs for Voice and Pianoforte* at Brett Young's own expense and purely for private circulation. This contained only two poems, of quite different mood from earlier selections: 'The Vagabond' from *Songs of Travel* by R.L. Stevenson (one of the writers whom Francis's mother read aloud to him when he was a child) and 'Almond, Wild Almond' by another contemporary poet, Herbert Trench (1865-1923). As the title suggested, 'The Vagabond' told of one who wandered freely, asking no more of life than the heaven above and the road below, just in fact the freedom that Owen Lucton would later seek, albeit only for a brief interlude. The essential message of Trench's poem was that the old songs were true: a sentiment which was to be very much at the heart of the majority of Brett Young's writing. 'Almond, Wild Almond' was included in the programme at Jessie's first song recital in the Grosvenor Room of the Grand Hotel, Birmingham, in February 1913, whilst four years earlier at a charity concert supporting Lowestoft fishermen, accompanied by her husband, she had sung Francis's arrangement of 'The Lamplighter' from Stevenson's *Child's Book of Verse*.

Though evidently happier employing the words of others for his musical talents, Brett Young composed at least one complete entity of both words and music with his 'River Serenade'. This poem's theme was the same as that which he had explored exhaustively through his selections from other poets and which Jim Redlake, at a similar stage in life, addressed to Cynthia Folville. It was, in fact, the very style of much of Brett Young's later verse: a somewhat senti-mentalised picture of lovers in Elysium.

> While the great pale moon is gleaming
> And its mellow light is streaming,
> Come along love, let's be dreaming
> On the river in its light...
> While the streamlet, softly creeping,
> Mingles with the river's weeping,
> Come along love, all is sleeping
> Neath the gentle shade of night.
> (FBY 93)

During these years, when a literary future remained a distant dream, Francis Brett Young seriously considered an alternative career in music. In his biography *My Life of Music*, Sir Henry Wood recalled Francis seeking his advice as to the possibility of his becoming a professional accompanist. Believing that this would take at least five years of concentrated practice, Wood advised against it, eventually being able to flatter himself when the novelist's reputation was established that readers of fiction might have lost many hours of pleasure but for his advice. However, for someone who had taught himself to play the piano only a few years earlier, Francis obviously displayed a not inconsiderable musical talent.

After months of planning, in which the churches of both Hales Owen and Alvechurch were eliminated as being too close to home, on Monday 28 December 1908, Francis Brett Young and Jessie Hankinson were married at the church of St Michael in the Mendip village of Rowberrow. Here generations of Bretts and Youngs had been baptised, married and buried, as Edwin Ingleby discovered on his visit to his father's relatives.

> In a little while they came to the church of Highberrow. It was
> a humble and not very beautiful building; but Edwin entered
> the churchyard with awe, for it seemed to him that so much
> of the past that had made him lay buried there.
> (YP 198)

Neither of the families had been told of the arrangements, though in anticipation of the event Dr Thomas Brett Young, 'in his stinginess, sent us a miserable £5-5. A man with £1800 a year to his eldest son!' (FBY 422). Jessie had been with her parents at Alvechurch on the very morning of the wedding. Meeting the two witnesses en route, she travelled by train to Bristol and met Francis just after midday. Then followed a thirty-mile drive through deep snow to Rowberrow for the ceremony conducted by the rector, Rev. J. Havelock Collins. Leo Hayes of the Octette was the best man and a friend from Rhoda Anstey's Training College, Elsie Poultney, who later ran The Leasowes as a country health farm, the sole bridesmaid. Bride and groom both wore Harris tweeds, and the only other member of the congregation was the verger. When Rev. Charles Pearson Rector of Halesby arrived for the marriage of Susan Lorrimer and Dick Pennington, 'the wedding-party awaited him; a small group, which consisted of the bride, the bridegroom, two witnesses and the verger' (MMP 166). Rev. Pearson's hope for the young couple who stood before him was that they would be faithful and happy and have a large family. Though Francis and Jessie undoubtedly did live faithfully and happily ever afterwards, they had no children, which must have proved a particular sadness in view of the hope expressed by the twenty-two-year-old Francis:

> I think I love children more than any of the other creatures that brighten the face of this weary globe. A child appeals to that wonderful protective sense which is the greatest crown of mankind. With God's help I shall be a better father than I have been son.
> (FBY 256)

Following a honeymoon spent at Skelwith Bridge, Westmorland, whilst Leo Hayes acted as locum at Cleveland House, the Brett Youngs returned to Brixham, where for a further five and a half years Francis led the busy life of a fishing port's doctor, his only permanent experience of general practice, which, with its ceaseless anxiety, restlessness and grinding physical toil, he found more demanding than he had anticipated. Medical training and experience were, however, the bases upon which Brett Young was to lay the foundations of his literary achievements.

> There is nothing in the world which so fits a man of letters to wrestle with the mind as an intimate acquaintance with the body. Literally and figuratively the doctor sees thousands of

men and women naked; he sees the spring of curious motives, he shares strange secrets. A man or woman will tell lies or feign emotions to the pastor or the lawyer. With the physician they know that only the truth will help them.
(FBY 973)

The experiences of Brett Young's G.P. heroes in *My Brother Jonathan* and *Dr Bradley Remembers* were graphic pictures of the very anxiety and grinding toil which their author himself lived through in Brixham. There he visited remote farmworkers (and their wives during their confinements), first in the dog-cart and then in the temperamental secondhand Rover which he had bought from his brother-in-law in order to keep pace with other Brixham doctors. Francis's adventures in this fantastic vehicle were repeated by Jonathan Dakers, whose newly-acquired car was a questionable aid to his house-calls.

> That motor-car was an offence to God and man, destroying the peace of every street it invaded with fumes of burnt oil and an exhaust that pounded like a water-hammer. If it were not over-lubricated it grew hot and gave up the ghost. Its radiator steamed like a samovar. The ignition was supplied through a commutator to which short-circuits were second nature. Its lion-hearted engine would 'negotiate' any ordinary hill, in time and with coaxing. Unfortunately, one or two of the Wednesford hills were extraordinary; the bottom gear was too high for them — and Jonathan was therefore forced to ascend them backwards in reverse.
> (MBJ 191)

Like Dr Quicke, Brett Young practised dentistry, extracting teeth at one shilling per tooth, or one and sixpence with local anaesthetic, a skill and rate of pay with which he endowed John Bradley.

> The doctor was a 'dab-hand at tooth-drawing'. One swift pounce, a look of terror, an agonised shriek that made the waiting-room shiver, and then Dr Bradley holding the trophy aloft in triumph: a cheap shillingsworth.
> (DBR 18)

The crews of the sailing ketches flocked to the New Road surgery during their shore leave, as Reuben Henshall once visited his doctor in Brixham. 'He sat on a bench in the waiting-room. The doctor's wife brought him a cup of tea with three lumps of sugar in the saucer. Torn copies of *Punch* littered the benches, and he read mechanically a joke about toothache' (DS 239).

Later psychology which would applaud the soothing effects of music played in medical waiting-rooms was anticipated (perhaps unintentionally) in Cleveland House, where patients could hear Jessie practising her singing in the music room as they waited for their appointment, or came to collect the prescriptions which were left on the surgery mantelpiece.

However, Francis's medical duties were not only routine. In 1912 one of his patients, a two-year-old girl, became seriously ill and Dr Brett Young diagnosed pneumonia and diphtheria, realising that the child's life was in grave danger. To the vexation of the matron, that this young doctor should admit an infectious patient into her charge, he transferred the girl, in his own car, to Brixham Cottage Hospital, where he successfully performed a tracheotomy. More than eighty years later Elsie Stabb, the very patient whose life the doctor had saved, was to unveil plaques on Brett Young's two homes in Brixham. Transposed to Wednesford, the incident of 1912 provided material for a scene in *My Brother Jonathan*, published in 1928.

> Nothing but a diphtheric membrane could have clogged the larynx like this, starving the lungs of the air that was life. Now it was only a matter of moments. One chance — a thin chance — and one only. Yes, there it was, thank heaven! A doubtful scalpel. And a number twelve rubber catheter. Anything would do. He sliced the rubber tube in half and approached the bed. No time for sterilisation. Lister be damned! He knelt by the bedside, bending over the child, the dubious scalpel poised like a pen in his fingers. Tracheotomy without chloroform! This was vivisection with a vengeance!
> (MBJ 202-203)

The Brixham experience found other reflections in *My Brother Jonathan*. Dr G. Blacker Elliott, Medical Officer of Health and first of the fishing port's practitioners to own a car, was the inspiration for Wednesford's Medical Officer Dr Craig, who during the course of the story exchanged his dog-cart for a motor-car. In Craig's partner, Dr Monaghan, 'a red-haired young man from the county of Kerry, with an enormous mouth from which a smile was never absent, and an ingratiating brogue', (MBJ 127) may be seen Brixham's genial, red-haired Southern Irish doctor C.B.P. Troy, whilst the rather acid matron of Brixham Cottage Hospital was no doubt in Brett Young's mind when he drew the dour, dessicated Miss Jessell, her counterpart at Wednesford.

However, *My Brother Jonathan* was one of the products of success, and in the Brixham years Brett Young still had to make his name. This was the period in which literary rejections were more common than acceptances. 'Miner of Axmoor', one of the first short stories Francis wrote, was never published. Another rather grim tale, 'Bridal of Korea', was returned by J.B. Pinker, Brett Young's newly-appointed agent, who did not think any magazine editor would accept it, for though interesting, it was too frank. (The story was eventually published by Cassell under the title of 'East is East'.) The receipt of Gertrude Dale's wholesale condemnation of his sixty thousand word first novel, *Isolde St Gabriel*, the story of a girl living with her disreputable father in a squalid coastal mansion, prompted Francis's admission that he had always had a sneaky sensation that it was bad. *At Zeal Ferry*, a second and longer novel with a similar Devon background, met with a similar reception. 'Roman's Folly', the short story begun on board the *Kintuck* and completed in Bloxwich seemed to Brett Young 'a church without a steeple, which wants loads of literary elbow grease to make it less dull' (FBY 367, 369).

The novelist Eden Phillpotts was more enthusiastic about 'Roman's Folly', anticipating that what he had done for Dartmoor Brett Young might do for Mendip. Another short story, 'Playground of Winds', also brought encouragement from Phillpotts, who saw in it a feeling for phrase and refinement of ideas as well as a rare sense of atmosphere. A further criticism provoked a response which gave insight into Brett Young's current literary state of mind.

> Robertson-Nichol has been reading 'Playground of Winds'. He says it is very well-written, but glum and unhappy. (Of course!) So much for the horrid Scotsman. Well if I can't write happy I can't.
> (FBY 443)

However, there were some successes: 'Furze Bloom', a moorland idyll set in the Mendips, became Brett Young's first-ever published short story; *Fry's Magazine* accepted 'Puppets at the Fair', a story which Francis admitted was written in atrocious English; Tillotsons accepted 'Birds of Passage' and 'Matrimonial'; whilst a poem, 'Sea Fancies', along with 'The Dead Village', a story of depopulation in the Mendips, was published by *The Thrush*. At this stage in his writing, it was still Francis's intention to set his works in the Mendips, from which his ancestors came. What Geoffrey Eyles was to do years later in his map of Brett Young's borderlands, published as endpapers to the best-selling Severn Edition, Francis anticipated doing for the Mendips while still unknown.

> Someday soon when the stories have increased — multiplied and replenished the earth, we will get a map of Mendip and label the places with their proper names. Highberrow, Roman's Folly, Great Barrow Farm and the rest.
> (FBY 369)

It was not to be a Mendip location which brought success to Brett Young's major literary efforts during these Brixham years. *The Young Physician*, begun in 1911 and *The Iron Age*, begun in 1914, both had Midland settings, whilst *Undergrowth*, published in 1913 and *The Dark Tower*, published in 1914, moved into the heart of the English-Welsh borderlands. Of *The Dark Tower*, which he originally intended to call *Trecastle*, Brett Young later remarked that he had never written, and did not suppose that he ever would write, a better book. Having been turned down by thirteen publishers, *Undergrowth*, seen by its authors as representing a new genre in literature, was finally accepted by Martin Secker, for whose series of 7/6d monographs the critical study *Robert Bridges* was commissioned. The other five novels written wholly or partly in Brixham (*The Tragic Bride* was written on Brett Young's return to the town during the Summer of 1919) also appeared under the same imprint.

The atmosphere of Brixham as Francis knew it was best captured in *Deep Sea*, published in 1914, the novel which told of the fishermen and salesmen and their wives with whom he was in daily contact. Some insight into the lives of such people was illustrated by Nesta and Jeffery Kenar's living room.

> The walls were adorned with pictures whose subjects had a very direct bearing upon the life of the people. One, a coloured map, quaintly marked with soundings, imaginary banks, shoals and submerged rocks, indicated its purpose by its title 'The Sailor's Chart through Life'. So minutely was Jeffery

Kenar acquainted with the set of currents in the Gulf of
Drunkenness, and the soundings of the Banks of Unbelief,
that he could have piloted the most waywardly inclined craft
through all its channels blindfold.
(DS 57)

Though the characters and incidents were imaginary, *Deep Sea*
remained a true story, with its Brixham family names: Kenar, Silley,
Parnall, Scoble, Crang; the period dialect: 'mazed'; 'go aisy'; 'fay';
'bunny' — the peculiarly Brixham substitute for a much stronger
expletive; the clock on the Co-op stores at the bottom of Sheepy Lane;
Reuben Henshall's boat the *Pilgrim*, named after the very fishing
smack which appeared as number BM45 in the 1911 Brixham Register
of vessels and their owners; and the annual Regatta.

In the middle of August the smacks set their restless sails and
steal back like a huge flight of homing pigeons. The deserted
anchorage becomes bright with the colours of canvas. The
streets are full of fishermen. Their wives throng the Fore Street
shops in search of dainties, and the children wake in the
morning to count their pennies. For this is the holiday of the
year, and on the flood of excited speech which eddies in every
street, floats the magic word 'Regatta'.
(DS 24)

The narrow lanes and alleys behind the harbour provided the
setting for houses suggesting the squalor which would be apparent
in the later Black Country novels.

Ruth's house was depressing beyond words. It faced the little
passage that led from the steps into the Stygian recesses of the
court, where the houses huddled one another as though they
only held their stones together by the centuries' accretion of
plaster and dirt.
(DS 266)

The storm, in which the *Pilgrim* was wrecked and Ruth widowed,
called to mind the tragedy of winter 1910 when four Brixham smacks
(*Eva*, *Speedwell*, *Vigilance* and *Marjorie*) were lost with all hands
during a heavy gale in the Bristol Channel.

The wind was very terrible that night; it swept through the
harbour as the rout of a lost battle. It beat on ramparts of

unyielding stone, tore at the slates, and howled in fury that it could not bend them. The cordage of the smacks in the basin sang with a rasping note: the water hissed below, and the gas lamps of the quay were all blown out, so that to the wind's tumult was added the horror of darkness. By the following evening the whole town knew that every vessel was accounted for save five: the *Pilgrim, Niobe, Deerhound, Ibis* and *Traveller.*
(DS 275, 283)

The increasing demands of Brett Young's writing career were indicated by the fact that shortly before the First World War he took on a partner, Dr Hosegood, the practice having become too much for one doctor-writer. It was at this point that Francis and Jessie left Cleveland House, moving out to the Old Garden House on Berry Head, with its magnificent views over Tor Bay and the English Channel and a garden filled with pink geraniums. Jane Hoare became housekeeper-caretaker and shared their home with the Siamese cats, Tosca and Pertif. Elsa, Mrs Willis's Siamese cat, 'an adorable sleekness of fur the colour of froth on storm-water', (IA 94) added reality to the ambience of *The Iron Age* as yet another indicator of Brett Young's recycled personal experiences.

The coming of war meant that the Brixham experience was almost at an end. It had not been a great financial success. Of the fourteen hundred pounds which patients owed to Francis after seven years of practice, only fourteen pounds was ever paid, leaving him much worse off than he left Dr Bradley, who was owed only four thousand pounds after fifty years of practice. Perhaps this explained why so much of Francis's subsequent correspondence with his agents and publishers focused upon their prompt payment of his royalties. These years, however, had fed Francis Brett Young's imagination with ideas that would find expression in his future writing, and for which his gratitude would be permanently recorded.

> The people of Brixham were a hardy, shrewd and generous race. I am proud to have lived among them and known them and to have been counted as their friend, and glad that I was able to put on record some aspects of a life which was singularly rich in colour and interest.
> (DS Preface viii)

Six: War

That night the world went mad. It was the fourth of August
in the year 1914.
   (PC 616)

Devastating effects of war hovered like spectres over Brett
Young's writings. The end of *The Iron Age*, first of the Mercian
novels, was rewritten to conclude with the rejoicing of industrialist
Walter Willis at his potential profits from the appetites of World War
One. The death of Edward Willis in the conflagration welcomed by
his father was reported in *Mr Lucton's Freedom*, last of the Mercian
novels, the closing pages of which were overshadowed by the coming
of World War Two. In the intervening novels, the Boer War and the
Great War were pivotal.

   Out of pride rather than conviction, Ralph Hingston volunteered
for the Imperial Yeomanry and died of enteric fever at Bloemfontein,
where Gerald Tregaron met an identical fate. Hugo Pomfret, having
survived the Boer War, succumbed to a stroke on the troop ship
which carried him home. A generation later his son Jasper was
killed at the Battle of Neuve Chapelle. Roger Ombersley perished at
Gheluvelt, whilst his brother Richard was claimed by the Somme,
where Captain Small was blown up and buried. Though Joe Small
survived, 'when he limped back with his mutilated body and
wretched pension, the stock of heroism had slumped and unem-
ployable heroes had become a nuisance' (MMP 22).

   With the outbreak of the First World War, Brett Young's doctor-
heroes volunteered for active service. Jonathan Dakers was refused,
panel doctors with long lists of patients being required at home. Too
old for war service, John Bradley became Commandant of Sedgebury Hospital where he dealt with the wreckage of war, whilst Major
Edwin Ingleby served as Registrar of Pedworth Military Hospital.

Their creator also volunteered, confident in his opinion that 'whatever ethical views the ordinary man may hold about war, for the doctor the issue is clear' (FBY 32).

So it was that on 1 January 1916 Francis Brett Young received his one-year commission as Lieutenant in the Royal Army Medical Corps. A course of officer-training, which he entered along with five other recruits, took place on Salisbury Plain. Under the command of Captain Sheedy, No. 2 Camp, Sling, about three miles from Stonehenge, where the menu offered beef for breakfast, lunch and dinner, and basic training comprised four hours of daily drill, did not excite Francis. 'There's no doubt but that Sling is a place wholly forsaken by God. We are four miles of mud from Tidworth, two miles of mud from Bulford' (FBY 456). The barracks at Sling were arranged in alphabetical order, Brett Young being billeted in 'Delhi', where he paid his orderly, a Worcestershire boy named Munn, half-a-crown a week. Typically, Francis was critical of those around him. Munn he dismissed as not very capable and Sheedy as most objectionable.

Despite his description of military routine as tomfoolery, Lieutenant Brett Young impressed his fellow officers by his keenness and the enthusiasm which he put into his training, shown in his eagerness to be the first to fall in on the parade ground. Life at Sling, however, was not all drill: still recovering from his own anti-typhoid inoculation, Francis received orders to march eighty men down to Bulford Hospital where he would inoculate them. Other duties were less suited to his natural inclinations.

> Yesterday being the ninth Sunday after nothing, I, who had innocently given my name as being Church of England, was detailed to take church parade. Quite a nice young padre (when he didn't turn his eyes heavenwards) preached on foul language.
> (FBY 461)

Once the day's duties were over, there was time to read (Balzac, Stendhal and Boswell) and to write, completing *The Iron Age* standing at the shelf in his room which held his typewriter.

Shortly after Francis's arrival at Sling, Jessie moved into the George Hotel, Amesbury, just as Clare accompanied Steven to Sling, an outpost of the permanent camp at Bulford on Salisbury Plain. The Officers' School of Instruction at Pedworth, a thinly disguised Tidworth, had similar alphabetical barracks (*Albuera, Blenheim,*

Corunna, Dargai) and a main road which was little more than a quagmire of unmetalled chalk. A decade later, the frenzied activities of Sling still lived in Brett Young's mind.

> On every 'square' bodies of men drilling heard the bark of staccato commands, the thud of grounded arms, the rhythmical tramp of heavy boots, the symphony of bugle-calls. The road was congested with troops route-marching, with convoys of grey-hooded lorries swaying over the uneven surfaces, with level-crossings of the military railway. A battery of howitzers crossed the road; great grey monsters with their mouths gaping at the sky, where fighting-planes went droning by like hornets.
>
> (PC 662-663)

Basic training complete, two false alarms suggested that Brett Young would be posted either to Madras or the Dardenelles. The indecisions of this time were recalled when Harold Dakers received his orders. '"Prepare for immediate embarkation for Madras." That was good. There was no war in Southern India' (MBJ 440). Short-lived relief was soon exchanged for dismay. 'There had been a mistake in orders. For "Madras" read "Mudros" — the medical base for the Dardenelles' (MBJ 443). On 31 March 1916, Francis Brett Young's uncertainties were resolved at Plymouth when he boarded the *RMSS Balmoral Castle* bound for Cape Town and service under General Smuts, in what would prove to be, geographically at least, the worst theatre of the war, the German East African Campaign.

While the *Balmoral Castle* lay in Plymouth Sound, Jessie's frantic requests for permission to accompany her husband to South Africa were refused by the Foreign Office and the ship sailed at 2 p.m. on Saturday 1 April. Perhaps the disappointment of separation caused Francis to describe those ladies who had been more successful in reaching Cape Town in the Boer War than had Jessie in the Great War as

> frivolous society women with the power to pull strings and get out there, simply to prey upon the husbands of women who are doing their duty in England.
>
> (PC 348)

Brett Young was one of approximately twenty medics aboard the *Balmoral Castle*. Though he considered his fellow passengers to be generally very dull, there were exceptions. Jesuit priest Father Garrould was the aspiring author of a single novel, *The Onion Peelers*; Governor of Mauritius Sir Hesketh Bell (who was accompanied by his aide) was writing his reminiscences. When Jim Redlake travelled from Cape Town to Durban, also aboard the *Balmoral Castle*, also in the company of a colonial governor and his aide, the ship was given over to a draft of twenty or more medical officers, life on board being vividly described.

> The liner's routine went on as though the war meant nothing, as if she still carried her usual crowds of passengers. After dinner the band played the trivial, sentimental tunes that accompany the leisurely digestive processes of life at sea.
> (JR 505)

This leisurely life allowed Francis to learn such useful Swahili phrases as *viboko sita vikale* (six savage hippopotami) and *one m'chizoke m'dogo* (find me a baby mongoose — female) from a Cowley Father who had spent years in German East Africa; and to work on his latest novel, the story of Abner Hackett, provisionally entitled *Food for Powder*. Distracted by the fact that he had received no reviews of *The Iron Age*, Francis made slow progress with this new work, eventually to be published in 1921 as *The Black Diamond*, the story of Abner Fellows. *Food for Powder* remained the title for an intended sequel to *The Black Diamond*, a proposed outline indicating a plot for which Leo Hayes' advice would be sought, but which was never developed.

> Abner Fellows in 1912; Process of discharge with a small pension. Where will he go: Halesby? Wolfpits? Back to army. Sergeant. Dreams of Egypt. That street in Alexandria. Parade Ground and football. The pub at Ludlow — with Edward Willis. N.B. from Leo: Process of discharge? After what service? Salisbury Plain; East African draft; Officer — one of the Delahays.
> (FBY 88)

During his brief stay in Cape Town, Brett Young visited the Rhodes Memorial at Groote Schuur before sailing for Mombassa on 21 April aboard the *Armadale Castle*, the conversion of which to auxiliary cruiser was graphically described in a letter to Jessie of May 1916.

First they gutted her. Bathrooms and lavatories were
scrapped wholesale: not because they took up room, but
because sanitation is evidently not considered necessary in
the tropics. We sleep, five of us, in an eight foot square, with
ports closed — a matter of light — and the temperature 85.
Everywhere on this ship the smell of humanity is appalling.
At night it filters through our close cabin, the only air that
reaches us is foetid, vitiated. In the morning one awakes with
a filthy mouth.
(FBY 479)

Even when Brett Young wrote his letters home, he was considering
their future value, indicating to Jessie that she should show them
both to his brother Eric and to Leo Hayes. Contemporary observation played a significant part in later writing. The description of the
evisceration of the *Armadale Castle* in which Jim Redlake sailed to
Mombassa, was almost a verbatim copy of this letter.

First of all they had gutted her. Bathrooms and lavatories had
vanished, not because they occupied space, but because clean-
liness and sanitation in the tropics were evidently regarded
by the navy as unnecessary luxuries. Jim found himself
crammed into a cabin eight feet square with five other
officers.... At night all lights were extinguished, all port-holes
closed. After breathing the air of the tween-decks for more
than an hour at a time Jim emerged on deck panting, with a
filthy mouth.
(JR 519, 524)

Congella Camp, Durban, allowed Brett Young a brief social life,
which privilege he also permitted Jim Redlake, who received invi-
tations to dances, tennis, picnics, surf-bathing and diversions of
every kind. However the stay was short, and the final leg of the
journey to Mombassa saw Francis working on the fiction of Abner
Fellows, by then grown old enough for a tentative love affair, whilst
reflecting upon the reality into which he himself was sailing.

I don't fear death in itself. I could perhaps even get a little
satisfaction out of the fact that what we are doing is our duty,
a plain thing, far removed from patriotic cant: nothing more
or less than the righting of a gross and obvious wrong.
(FBY 480)

After docking in Mombassa on 8 May, Brett Young travelled via the
Uganda Railway to Nairobi, where he anticipated being stationed at

the Indian Hospital. Within less than a week however, he was appointed Medical Officer to the Second Rhodesian Regiment and was on his way to the front.

Sixteen months earlier, Colonel Paul von Lettow-Vorbeck had arrived in East Africa, the jewel of the German colonial empire, to take command of two thousand German officers and twenty thousand native askaris. He was charged with defending thousands of square miles of bush so dense, that one army might march past another without either realising. Fortunately for von Lettow, Allied High Command had failed to appreciate the difficulties of waging war in this land where the greatest enemies were climate, geography and disease, and had deployed only a North Lancashire battalion, a small force of Punjabis and limited East African troops.

For two years von Lettow held the initiative. Then in February 1916, England's old enemy from the Boer War, Jan Christian Smuts, was gazetted Lieutenant General in the British army and sailed for Mombassa to take charge of the East Africa campaign, with a polyglot army of troops from the United Kingdom, South Africa, Gold Coast, Nigeria, Rhodesia, Uganda, West Indies, the Indian sub-continent, Belgium and Portugal, supplemented by Boers, Arabs, the Cape Corps and the King's African Rifles native troops. Altogether 114,000 allied troops would fight in this campaign which cost a staggering seventy-two million pounds. Well-trained and deployed though the enemy undoubtedly was, Smuts' principal battle was against the country itself. His army was marching where no one had ever been before, in a climate which only native Africans could withstand. In 1916, out of 58,000 allied troops in German East Africa, 50,000 contracted malaria and the overall incidence of disease casualties to battle casualties throughout the campaign was thirty to one.

Smuts' initial aim was to drive the German forces from Kilimanyaro into the fever-swamps of the Pangani. Concentrating his attack on the five-mile Taveta gap between the foothills of Kilimanjaro and the northern extremity of the Pare Mountains, on 9 March, just before the rainy season which would hinder his advance for two months, he secured the town of Taveta, where Francis Brett Young arrived, after a thirty-six hour rail journey, on 17 May 1916.

There Francis made the acquaintance of the officer in charge of transport, Captain McQueen, who had lost his left arm in the charge of a wounded elephant, and whose phenomenal knowledge of Equatorial Africa had already proved invaluable in the campaign, in which he had been awarded the Military Cross. A month later McQueen, originally from the Isle of Skye, would report to the Field Ambulance with a broken collar-bone, in which sorry state he first appeared as Hector M'Crae in *The Crescent Moon*, a character who had also lost his left arm to a wounded elephant, and whose story was told in great detail. The commander of Jim Redlake's machine-gun company, a one-armed Scotsman named Macdiarmid, also had his origins in McQueen. Having purchased tinned food, cocoa and tea for the forthcoming advance, Francis consulted McQueen as to essential equipment and was advised to take six bottles of whisky and half a dozen boxes of oysters, as it would be delicacies that he would want at the front.

Four days after Brett Young arrived at Taveta, Smuts' plan to expel the German forces from the Pare and Usambara mountains, and to gain control of the Tanga Railway, was put into operation. The Second Brigade, under General Hannyngton, advanced directly down the Tanga line; the King's African Rifles set out through the mountains, hoping to attack the enemy from behind; along the east bank of the Pangani moved General Sheppard's East African Brigade, including the eight hundred strong Rhodesia Regiment under Colonel Essex Capell, who would feature in *Jim Redlake* as Colonel Essex. After an initial fifty-mile march westwards, the Brigade turned to the south, making camp at Soko Nassai. Six days later, having progressed seventy-five miles through some of the most difficult terrain imaginable, the enemy had still not been sighted.

> All the thick bush through which we passed was floored with loose sandy soil which rose in dense clouds, filling our eyes and blackening our parched lips. The pioneers' road twisted interminably between hacked tree-stumps: for the shortest way of penetrating bush of this kind is to take a rough bearing and follow the line of least resistance.
> (MT 59)

During the march from Soko Nassai to Old Lassiti Brett Young first encountered General Smuts, whom he greatly admired. Though suspected by his own countrymen, the charismatic 'Slim Jannie' commanded the devotion both of Jim Redlake and his creator. If Brett Young's assessment of his commander-in-chief was adulatory —

> The personality of that man dominated the whole conduct of the war in East Africa. If fortune had not carried him through the risks he faced daily, we should have lacked the enormous

psychical asset which his masterful courage gave us, and endured our deprivations and sickness with a less happy confidence.

(MT 238-239)

— then Jim Redlake's was positively idolatrous:

This man was not merely a human being but a cause and a will incarnate. His bodily presence revived Jim's faith and steeled his spirit to new endurance. Under this man's command he was ready and willing to subject himself to any conceivable torture or mutilation, to welcome death itself as a glorious sacrifice.

(JR 569)

This was an adoration which Brett Young was quite happy to communicate to its object, writing to thank General Smuts for the loan of his war diaries, used in researching *Jim Redlake*, 'I think you will find the details of the campaign pretty accurate and the experience of the central figure faithful to what most of us regimental officers were feeling during that stirring adventure' (FBY 2228).

Soon after encountering Smuts, Brett Young came under fire for the first time and had opportunity to test his devotion. On 29 May, in the bush near Mikocheni, the East African Brigade was bombarded by the 4.1" shells of the high-velocity guns rescued from the cruiser *Konigsberg*, which had been forced ashore in East African waters. At Buiko, the Rhodesian Regiment was overtaken by its original Medical Officer, and Brett Young ordered back to Nairobi, a bitter disappointment after this march of over one hundred and fifty miles,

one of the most extraordinary military feats that Africa has ever known, achieved through a country often waterless, often clogged with the most impenetrable bush, over roads, through zones that presented unknown difficulties.

(FBY 1688)

Convinced that in wartime the only place to be was at the front, Brett Young's request for a change of orders was granted and he was attached to Combined Field Ambulance Unit B120 (India Section), serving also as Brigade Sanitary Officer. Here Francis began to write his account of the campaign, published by Collins as *Marching on Tanga* in 1917.

1. Francis Brett Young in the Study of Craycombe House

2. The Laurels, Hales Owen. Francis Brett Young's birthplace

3. Dr. Thomas Brett Young's Consulting Room at The Laurels

4. The Drawing Room at The Laurels

5. Francis Brett Young, aged 2

6. Staff of No 6 Indian Hospital, Nairobi 1916. Francis Brett Young (middle row, 2nd left) nursing 'Billi', his serval cat. (From an original taken with Francis Brett Young's own camera and inscribed by him on the back.)

7. Esthwaite Lodge, now Hawkshead Youth Hostel

8. The Library, Craycombe House

9. Craycombe House Drawing Room

10. Craycombe House, near Fladbury, Worcestershire

11. Talland House, Talland Bay, Cornwall

12. Lounge at Montagu. Cathleen Mann portrait on the wall

13. Brett Young's South African home at Montagu

14. Francis Brett Young at his desk, Craycombe House

The East Africa experience also encouraged Francis to write verse, which, though unconvinced of its worth, he hoped Secker would publish.

> They form a kind of emotional commentary to the Tanga book. They are just intimate personal things which I was ashamed to say in prose, although probably I could have said them in prose so much better.
> (FBY 1697)

Though Robert Bridges found the poems of *Five Degrees South*, only three hundred copies of which were published, admirable and full of promise, other critics thought them awkward and stilted. A larger volume *Poems 1916-1918* was brought out three years later by Collins. Where the verse did not describe the immediate situation in which Brett Young found himself, it spoke both of what he had left behind: principally Jessie:

> It is not hope, nor faith
> That here my spirit sustaineth, but love only...
> I would have you know that your kiss
> Was more to me than all my hopes of infinity.
> (FDS 46)

and England:

> Marching on Tanga, marching the parch'd plain,
> Of wavering spear-grass past Pangani River,
> England came to me...
> (FDS 14)

and the isolation of Equatorial Africa:

> High on the tufted baobab-tree
> To-night a rain-bird sang to me
> A simple song, of three notes only,
> That made the wilderness more lonely...
> (FDS 18)

Memories of England were sustained by Brett Young's sole reading matter during the campaign, the *Oxford Book of Verse* and a small-scale map of England, the mountains and meadowlands of which he repeatedly travelled in imagination.

Leaving Buiko, the Brigade crossed to the west bank of the Pangani, where on 9 June Brett Young's section was ordered to join a flying column under Colonel Dyke of the 130th Baluchis, and advance on M'Kalamo. Here, escaping from heavy fire, Francis and fourteen companions, some of whom were already wounded and with but one rifle between them, were lost for twenty-four hours in bush

> as dense as any I had seen in Africa, and almost entirely of thorn. There was only one way of penetrating it: to lower one's head, sheltered by the wide helmet, and dive through, heedless of torn clothes or flesh.
>   (MT 143)

Despite frantic attempts to rejoin the main force, Francis maintained his British paternalism, explaining to a wounded sepoy that the relationship between them was that of a father and his children. He also managed to begin his longest poem to emerge from this experience, 'Testament'.

> If I had died, and never seen the dawn
> For which I hardly hoped, lighting this lawn
> Of silvery grasses; if there had been no light,
> And last night merged into perpetual night;
> I doubt if I should ever have been content
> To have closed my eyes without some testament
> To the great benefits that marked my faring
> Through the sweet world.
>   (FDS 24)

At Kilimanyaro, Francis acquired an orphaned serval kitten, which he loved dearly and named Billi. This savage creature was gradually tamed and remained his constant companion until November, when ill-health required that it be put down. After taking part in the combined attack on Handeni, which fell on 19 June, Francis joined the 2nd Kashmir Rifles to secure the Morogoro road, and in three days had reached the Lukigura River. However, the night spent in the bush at M'Kalamo had taken its toll.

> To-night I lay with fever in my veins
> Consumed, tormented creature of fire and ice,
> And, weaving the enhavock'd brain's device,
> Dreamed that for evermore I must walk these plains

98

Where sunlight slayeth life.
(FDS 21)

On 24 June Brett Young was ordered back to Handeni Hospital, where he remained for two weeks, occupying first, like Jim Redlake, a whitewashed room that had once been a prison cell in the castle, then a tent in the grounds, before returning to Lukigura Camp and joining the advance to Makindu.

Surrounded on three sides by German forces, the allied troops were tired and sick: sometimes up to three hundred were in the care of the field ambulance. Continuous enemy bombardment took a heavy toll.

All through that day of battle the broken sound
Of shattering Maxim fire made mad the wood;
So that the low trees shuddered where they stood,
And echoes bellowed in the brush around.
(FDS 38)

This, in Brett Young's opinion, was the most devastating act in the whole theatre of war in which he was involved; and it was there that his combatant role came to an end, when on 1 August, less than three months after his arrival in East Africa, a victim of dysentery and malaria, he began the journey back to Handeni. Jim Redlake and Arthur Martock, a temporary medical officer, who carried with him a battered portable typewriter on which he was writing a novel about the Black Country and the Welsh Marches, and whose malaria ended his East African service, were also evacuated from Handeni. At the Tanga railhead at Korogwe, they encountered the same delays as their creator, awaiting the iron freight-trucks which would take them on to Taveta and the Base Hospital at Voi, before transfer by mail-train to Nairobi, where Francis entered Lady Colville's Nursing Home.

Discharged on 26 August as fit for light duty, he took charge of a unit of the Indian General Hospital. In October, Francis was temporarily seconded to Maharajah Scindia of Gwalior's convalescent home for officers about six miles out of Nairobi, but neither of these responsibilities interrupted his writing. At the end of August he had dispatched to England the first half of *Marching on Tanga*, with which he confessed some disappointment, wondering if he would not be better to abandon it for *The Black Diamond*. However, when the news came that the *Tanga* script, of which he had no complete duplicate, had gone down on the P & O Liner *Arabia*, Brett Young was in no doubt as to his response. 'This leaves me some forty or fifty pages to rewrite. It's a horrible thing to face: this renewal of labour when the heat of composition has passed' (FBY 530).

Even as the rewriting was in progress, Francis began work on a violent African melodrama, originally to be called *Far Forests* or *House of the Moon* (Njumba ya Mweze), but eventually published as *The Crescent Moon*. This was intended to satisfy the American public, and to be both a 'shocker' and a sentimental romance with hero, heroine, villain and comic relief. 'Early this morning just as the sun was ri-i-sing, I started a new novel, all about Eva Burwarton and her brother James, the missionary, and Charles Hare (alias M'Crae) and Herr Godovius' (FBY 528).

As Arthur Martock waited for his year's contract to expire, he felt quite justified in openly expressing his opinion of the war. In a similar situation, Francis Brett Young's views changed. In July 1916, he had expressed the opinion that not being at the front was not quite right; by October, though admitting the vileness of war, he remained convinced that this particular war would make many men not only fitter, but better and wiser. By January 1917, his release now long overdue, the whole war had become a ghastly and criminal mistake, prolonged only out of simple vindictiveness. Coming to the conclusion that war was the last resort of human folly and bestiality, his final assessment of the world in which such conflagration was possible spoke of 'A sick planet driven mad with haste and plunging towards the particular perdition which later revealed itself and overwhelmed us all together' (FBY 23).

After a number of false alarms suggesting he would escort the 98th Infantry to Egypt, and a riding accident when his mount tripped in an ant-hole whilst chasing zebra, causing a double dislocation of Francis's forearm (relived two years later when Edwin Ingleby treated a Colles fracture of the ulna and radius in the Casualty Department of Prince's Hospital) he eventually sailed for Egypt. In an identical manner, Jim Redlake accompanied the Loyal North Lancs, aboard the *Desna*, upon the first leg of his journey back to England. The East African campaign continued after the departure of Captain Brett Young in January 1917, when Smuts also left; Brett Young for Bristol and convalescence and Smuts for a conference in London, where he became a member of the War Cabinet. Though he had succeeded in evicting German forces from the most fertile areas of the colony, guerrilla-like resistance continued until von Lettow (by then a general and, in later years, a personal friend of Smuts) received news of the Armistice and surrendered on 14 November 1918.

Arriving in England, Francis was given three weeks leave, which he spent in Brixham. Here, reunited with Jessie, the theme of his poetry was obvious.

> Was ever a moment meeter made for love?
> Beautiful are your close lips beneath my kiss;
> And all your yielding sweetness beautiful —
> Oh, never in all the world was such a night as this!
> (P 10)

A course of electrical treatment for his injured arm was prescribed at the Military Hospital, Devonport, where Jessie was a masseuse. Harold Dakers, who would also return home with a paralysed arm, received similar therapy. 'Martock prescribed electricity, together with massage and passive movements. It was a wonderful bit of luck to find a qualified masseuse on the spot' (MBJ 549). Brief spells of 'light duties' at various other hospitals followed in rapid succession, with Jessie, who had resigned from her job at Devonport, accompanying him whenever possible, packing or unpacking fourteen times. Finally Francis was appointed Registrar at the Military Hospital at Tidworth, where the C.O., realising that he was ill, sent him to convalesce in Ireland, the experiences of which appeared in *The Tragic Bride*.

Roscarna, Clonderriff, Lough and Slieve Annilaun, evoked the rural Ireland of Galway, 'Joyce's Country' (home of Biddy Joyce and the book's rustic characters), that wild and barren area of limestone mountains and deep ravines from Iar Connaught, west of Lough Corrib to Killary Harbour. From Galway, Gabrielle Hewish travelled to Dublin, through the Bog of Allen, wearing her best clothes of Connemara homespun, made by Monoghan, the tailor at Oughterard, where at the time of Brett Young's convalescence, John P. Monoghan was Justice of the Peace.

The Dublin of *The Tragic Bride* is the area south of the Liffey, bounded by College Green, where Gabrielle met Lt Radway at the gates of Trinity College; Grafton Street, where she enjoyed her first ice-cream at Mitchell's Tea Rooms; Kildare Street, where Gabrielle and her father stayed in the sole hotel; Baggot Street, where her grandmother kept one among a whole range of shops; and St Stephen's Green, location of the Shelbourne Hotel, where her wealthy relatives, the Halbertons stayed. In Dublin Francis and Jessie encountered Maud Gonne, subject of Yeats' love poetry, and, at the home of George Russell, better known as poet and painter, 'A.E.', members of Sinn Fein.

Back at Tidworth Brett Young met William Armstrong, with whom he wrote *The Furnace*, a play based on *The Iron Age*, first produced at Liverpool Playhouse in 1928. He also began a series of plays with W. Edward Stirling, director of Plymouth Repertory Theatre. Their first venture, a version of *The Crescent Moon*, was never staged, though a version by Brian Brooke was produced at Hofmeyr Hall, Cape Town, in 1948. Later works, however, met with more success. *The Third Sex* (subsequently *Powder Puff*), a modernisation of *The Taming of the Shrew*, first performed at Plymouth, starring Marie Robinson, moved to the Gaiety Theatre Manchester, as did *Captain Swing*, based on *The Village Labourer* by J.L. and Barbara Hammond. *Crepe de Chine*, at Plymouth, was a great success, with as many as four hundred people turned away from a full house in one night. *One of the Family* played at Manchester and the collaboration also produced *The Flame*, an adaptation of *The Dark Tower* in an Italian setting.

However this was not a happy partnership; Brett Young criticised both his partner's acting ability: '*Captain Swing* played extraordinarily well in Manchester, though Stirling and his wife were blots on the excellent cast', (FBY 765) and his presumption in claiming an undeserved role in the creative process.

> His share in *Crepe* was suggesting that a play, to be topical, should deal with a demobilised soldier. I wrote the first act, having invented every character. Then we talked things over and I wrote the other two. With regard to *Powder Puff*, the title was Stirling's as also the idea: I invented every situation and wrote every word. *Captain Swing* was my idea from beginning to end. *The Flame* was also my own idea: so much for Stirling's share in the work.
>
> (FBY 824)

Dismissing Stirling as an unknown second rate actor, Francis betrayed his prejudice with the comment, 'he is not a bad fellow but he is an actor and a Jew' (FBY 821).

A blatantly obvious dislike of all things Jewish frequently appeared in Brett Young's writing. Like his paternalism toward native Africans, this may merely have united him with the culture, class and attitude of his age. Alternatively, it may have been the disturbing trait of unrestrained anti-Semitism at which *Mr & Mrs Pennington* hinted. The narration of this novel, where only the author spoke, underlined how Jewish origins contributed to the defective character of Harry Levison. 'Excitement made him employ a Jewish excess of gesture. All the grossness of the middle-aged Jew was inherent in his carefully-tailored figure' (MMP 472, 489). The most insulting remark Susan Pennington could conjure with which to dismiss her erstwhile lover was, 'You rotten, mean little Jew!' (MMP 490). Captain Small's views extended beyond the individual to the race. 'Doesn't it make you see red to watch those Yids strutting about? They're the curse of the country. Remember what happened in Russia! Jews, every one!' (MMP 29).

The description of one of Eugene Dakers' creditors as 'an ill-shaven little Hebrew named Greenberg', (MBJ 88) added nothing to the plot of *My Brother Jonathan* unless it were the implication that Jews were, by definition, unsavoury. Virginia Tregaron mocked her sister's suitor Louis Wiener, as either her Semitic friend or her Hebrew admirer, whilst her father, when offered financial advice by Otto Wiener, resented the suggestion that he could possibly have anything in common with a Jew. One of Budge Garside's assistants at his boxing booth at Dulston Wake was disparagingly referred to as a Hebrew and even that likeable 'Autolycus', Isaac Meninsky, was dismissed as an odd little Cockney Jew.

> Kate Willoughby's physical characteristics were a positive hindrance: so dark as to make one suspect a Jewish descent, wholly unattractive to men, marked out, from the day of her birth, for perpetual spinsterhood.
> (CB 207)

Indeed Jewishness was spurned even by Jews themselves. Mr Morris aroused Harry Levison's sympathy because 'it was sad, he thought: you could guess the poor fellow's race if you saw nothing else' (MMP 426). Louis Wiener succeeded in banishing his feelings of racial identity, even if his appearance betrayed him: 'Although he looked like a Jew, he never spoke, or (what was much more important) felt like one' (HUW 171). Mr Marx, the Shipping Agent in Naples, was, in his own assessment, 'not a philanthropist; not even a Christian; but a damned fat old German Jew' (SH 34).

Though all these descriptions appeared in the fictional works of his own little world, Brett Young's reflection upon England's apathy concerning the treatment of Jews in Nazi Germany did not.

> To persecute the Jew
> Is vile; but lots of us are Aryans too,
> And understand.
> (I 441)

The portrayal of Jews throughout his writing qualified Brett Young's final view: not a sorrowful reflection upon the failings of his countrymen; rather a distasteful expression of a personal opinion.

Seven: Capri

Almost a year after Major Francis Brett Young was demobilised at the end of World War One, he decided to give up medicine and to live off the proceeds of his writing. Two factors influenced his consequent departure from England. The first was the need to seek a warmer climate to counteract the malaria which he had contracted whilst in East Africa; the second was the equally imperative necessity to live where the meagre earnings of a rising novelist would be sufficient. On the advice of Martin Secker, who believed that the island would be good not only for Brett Young's health, but also for his pocket, the decision was made to move to Capri.

Compton Mackenzie, always helpful to those who needed his aid, was already established on the island, and so his advice was sought. A prompt reply brought details of Rosaio, a charming little villa in Anacapri, which Edwin Cerio was prepared to let for sixty lire a month. If this were unacceptable, Mackenzie suggested his own casetta on the Piccola Marina which would be ten degrees warmer than Anacapri and would cost only fifty lire a month. As the exchange rate was currently thirty-five lire to the pound, Brett Young's limited financial resources would be equal to the expense.

'Little' was obviously an adjective appropriate to Rosaio, which comprised just three rooms: a bedroom, a sitting room and a kitchen, the whole villa having a domed roof and opening into a small rose-garden. However, Francis and Jessie were captivated by Mackenzie's letter, which included 'pictures of vine-wreathed pergolas and white Saracen roofs against a background of gleaming mountain-side. The little place looked ravishing' (MURC - VF 06.1929).

Though George Bernard Shaw, with whom Brett Young discussed the proposed move, was unimpressed, complaining that people only went to Capri to elope, the decision was made which would

105

establish the pattern for the next decade and a half, of winters spent in Italy and summers in England. Late in 1919, 'laden with mosquito-nets and insect-powders we set out and sat up (second-class) for two days and nights on the journey from London to Naples' (MURC - VF 06.1929). Many Brett Young characters would take a similar time over the identical journey and be equally captivated by the beauty of this enchanted island. After an evening departure from London, Ernest Wilburn reached Capri by the morning steamer three days later. Bella Tinsley saw from Naples

> an expanse of glittering sea embosomed in mountains, and in the midst of it — more like a lovely shape carved out of blue cloud than a piece of ponderable earth — there lay, or rather seemed to float dreamily on the waves, an island.
> (WL 363)

Brett Young's first arrival on the island was less glamorous.

> We arrived at Capri in the midst of the heaviest thunderstorm I have experienced. The main street ran like a salmon river and the road to Mackenzie's romantic house was clogged with tenacious mud. From the little Piazza Caprile we walked down a stream of rushing water to Rosaio.
> (FBY 25)

Something of this wild weather was recalled when honeymooners Clare and Ralph Hingston arrived on the island, following a crossing which had confined the sea-sick bridegroom to his cabin.

> The roar of the sea encompassed them; the mountain-tops were stripped by a gale that seemed an extension of the loud sea's savagery. The inhabitants of the island kept closed doors.
> (PC 267)

The potential of this savage climate symbolised a different aspect of the character of the carefree, agrarian natives of the island, 'a kindly, industrious peasantry; the true owners of Capri: the tillers of the soil, the treaders of grapes and gatherers of olives' (WL 366-367). These very Capresi, however, also trapped quails by blinding a captured bird so that its cries attracted the flocks of spring migrants into their nets. Brett Young's view of the industry was ambivalent. Through the wider context of cynical fatalism, 'The Quails', reminiscent of his earlier 'Bête Humaine' and amongst the most popular of his verse in poetry anthologies, attempted to come to terms with the callous slaughter, the culinary results of which he most certainly enjoyed.

> Why should I be ashamed? Why should I rail
> Against the cruelty of men? Why should I pity,
> Seeing that there is no cruelty which men can imagine
> To match the subtle dooms that are wrought against them
> By blind spores of pestilence: seeing that each of us,
> Lured by dim hopes, flutters in the toils of death
> On a cold star that is spinning blindly through space
> Into the nets of time?
> (GP 198-199)

At the Piazza Umberto I, in the island's capital, Brett Young discovered the hub of Capri society. To the north lay the Bay of Naples; the steep road from the harbour passed through the square as it climbed up to Anacapri; to the south, steps led up to the seventeenth century Church of Santo Stefano. It was from this vantage point that Harriet Mortimer and Bella Tinsley took stock of their surroundings.

> The little piazza lay open towards the sea and commanded one of the most spectacular views in Christendom. Beneath, the fertile levels of Capri, their brown vineyards dotted with white-washed roofs and straw-screened orange-groves; beyond these, the incredible limestone bastion of Monte Solaro concealed the drift of domed cottages called Anacapri.
> (WL 375)

The Parish Church of Santo Stefano, 'a dank building which smelt of dirt mingled with incense and malodorous gloom', (WL 375) which Francis misleadingly designated a cathedral, (a status it had not enjoyed since 1816, when the Bourbon King Ferdinand IV re-established his court at Naples, following Napoleon's defeat at Waterloo) did not meet with the approval of either Miss Mortimer or Mr Pomfret. Having attended a service, Aunt Harriet emerged, a mixture of anxiety and distress.

> 'I couldn't stay there another minute. The air was suffocating.

107

There was a dreadful old woman who insisted on crowding up against me.'

'My aunt has been to the cathedral,' Bella said.

Pomfret laughed. 'I can quite understand how she feels in that case.'

(WL 378)

Anacapri, the only other town of any size on the island, at an altitude of 286 metres, a place of oriental aspect surrounded by vineyards was, as Bella Tinsley confirmed, much quieter than the capital. 'The streets of the mountain village were deserted. The roar of the blanched olive-groves enveloped it like the sound of the sea' (WL 383). Such natural peace prompted Francis's appreciation of Secker's recommendation. 'You were right in preferring the mountain simplicity of Anacapri rather than Capri itself, which is a mixture of greenhouse and theatre' (FBY 1724).

High above Anacapri, Clare and Ralph Hingston gained their view of some of the island's eight hundred species of flora from the craggy slopes of Monte Solaro.

> The lower slopes of the mountain were dusted with peach-blossom of so ethereal a pink that it seemed to hang among the dark foliage of orange-trees and loquats like a suspended flight of butterflies. As they climbed higher, there rose to meet them a savour, hot, pungent, aromatic, issuing from myrtle, lentisk, rush and creeping rosemary. Bramble and bracken straggled down; the turf was dappled with sturdy orchis, with blood-red uprights and velvety purple falls; cascades of lithospermum, bluer than Ralph's eyes.
>
> (PC 270)

Rosaio, set in a garden of trailing vines and abundant flowers among the olive groves of Anacapri, cost Francis all of seven and sixpence a week, with linen, silver and china included. The villa had previously been home to Compton Mackenzie, who had written the second volume of *Sinister Street* whilst living there. Until the month prior to Brett Young's arrival, Rosaio was occupied by the Italian composer Ottorino Respighi, who had arranged Rossini's music for the ballet, *La Boutique Fantasque* during his time there. Rosaio's artistic associations were later to be continued when Graham Greene became the owner. Here Francis and Jessie lived a simple life, like the islanders taking the sun as their only clock, mornings being given over to work and the rest of the day to leisure. As Mackenzie had moved to the opposite end of the island, the wisdom of his settling Brett Young in Rosaio was obvious: neither impinged upon the other's territory. Later recollections introduced confusion over the Brett Youngs' first residence on Capri. According to Francis, they moved straight to Rosaio, after calling on Compton Mackenzie, whom they had expected to meet them on arrival. 'He didn't; but he did the next best thing which was to send his gardener. Our house was all ready: a servant had been engaged; the gardener would take us up to Anacapri' (MURC - VF 06.1929). Mackenzie's opinion, however, was that Cerio had been making some alterations at Rosaio, which were not completed in time for Brett Young's arrival. As a consequence Mackenzie's offer of his own casetta (which consisted of two sparsely-furnished rooms over a boathouse) on the Piccola Marina was accepted, with Cerio supplying sufficient furniture to make the place habitable until Rosaio was ready.

Certainly Francis and Jessie did move to the Piccola Marina, though Francis's memory suggested that the removal did not happen for some time, and not for the reason recalled by Mackenzie.

> I, on my mountain settled down to write *The Black Diamond* until November and with it, gales and torrents. If Bernard Shaw could have seen Rosaio then, with its dank walls, its dishevelled pergolas and its smoking fire of wet olive-wood, before which we sat facing the alternatives of freezing or asphyxiation, he wouldn't have chosen it as a place to elope to.
> (MURC - VF 06.1929)

Again Compton Mackenzie, grand puppeteer of the island's literati, came to the rescue:

> I told him that if something wasn't done we should freeze to death in Rosaio and remain there, forgotten. Mackenzie, generous as ever, immediately sent us the key of a cottage at the Piccola Marina.
> (MURC - VF 06.1929)

James Money, in his copious social history, *Capri, Island of Pleasure*, suggested yet a third alternative to the beginning of the Brett Youngs' life on the island, placing them rent-free for several weeks at Weber's Strand-pension. Only when Francis's writing had generated some income did they pay Weber's bill, before moving into Rosaio.

The arrival of the impecunious Drogo D'Abitot on an unnamed island in 'True Blue' and the credit he received on the strength of his tales of lost luggage and aristocratic connections were, no doubt, recollections of the way in which the hospitable residents of Capri welcomed those whom they took to themselves.

Rosaio, however, was only a short-term lease. Brett Young's permanent home on Capri was to be Villa Fraita, rented from Antonino Mazzarella who lived nearby. It was his involvement in the Naples trial and acquittal of Alfredo Mazzarella in 1931 which was to provide Francis with material for a future novel.

> *Mr and Mrs Pennington* is a true story, although the events took place in Italy. It cost me over £100 to defend the unfortunate youth and I gave evidence of his character at the trial.
> (FBY 2270)

Fraita, a small pleasant villa which had the luxury of electric light instead of oil lamps and candles, was set in olive groves which swept from mountain to sea. The addition of a grand piano, imported from Naples, made the paradise complete. Having made the decision that he would like to remain on Capri for longer than he had originally intended, the climate suiting his health and the cost of living his pocket, Francis decided to buy Fraita when it came onto the market. A lack of funds was met by Compton Mackenzie with the loan of twenty-five thousand lire, a debt which was quickly repaid, thanks to the payment by *Metropolitan Magazine* of three hundred pounds for the American serial rights of *The Tragic Bride*.

Architect Edwin Cerio became involved with the redecoration of Fraita, in July 1925 submitting plans complete with drawings of goldfish swimming in a pond, which outlined the addition of a fountain and pool at the entrance to the villa's patio, and all for the cost of between two and three hundred lire! This was part of an agreement under which Brett Young was to translate eleven chapters of Cerio's somewhat rabelasian tale, *That Capri Air* and to write the foreword to the English edition. (The remaining four chapters were translated by Louis Golding, Norman Douglas and Richard Reynolds.)

During an immensely productive period on Capri, Brett Young worked on thirteen novels. Strangely, in that stunningly beautiful

Italian landscape overlooking the Tyrrhenian Sea, his thoughts frequently returned to the scarred face of his native Black Country for plots and stories.

> The England for which I feel most tenderly is the Black Country. It may not be particularly beautiful, but it is the very heart of England and the people who inhabit it and speak its language are the soundest, kindliest and toughest to be found.
> (FBY 62)

Two novels set in the Black Country were dedicated to fellow emigrants: *The Black Diamond*

TO
M. COMPTON MACKENZIE
GRATEFULLY: AFFECTIONATELY

and *Cold Harbour* to

Amico suo
Axel Munthe,
Medicus scriptori:
Scriptor medico.

When Cassell (to whom he had briefly transferred from Collins, his publishers during the early Capri years) wished to bring out the 270,000 word *Portrait of Clare* in two volumes, Francis expressed an opinion which he would probably have preferred to hide from his readers. 'I am convinced that to divide it is not only artistically (which doesn't particularly matter) but commercially wrong' (FBY 956). The result of this decision was that Brett Young began the successful alliance with Heinemann which was to last for the rest of his life, having first assured himself that his new publishers were aware that he transferred to them not as 'an author on whom they have to make a hazardous speculation, but as a safe and steady seller' (FBY 964). Both of these decisions regarding *Portrait of Clare* proved to be right. It was this novel which marked the beginning of Brett Young's financial success and sealed his public recognition, with the award of the James Tait Black Memorial Prize, an annual award shared by a novelist and a biographer. *Portrait of Clare* received the prize as the best novel of 1927, whilst H.A.L. Fisher won the biography prize for his two-volume study of James Bryce.

Other stories from the Capri years with Black Country settings were *My Brother Jonathan; Jim Redlake; Mr & Mrs Pennington; The House Under The Water* and *This Little World*. The five remaining novels were *The Red Knight; Sea Horses; Black Roses* (a story told to Francis by Edwin Cerio, *who knows what really happened*, to whom the novel was dedicated); *Woodsmoke* and *The Key of Life*.

What Francis actually achieved in these thirteen novels did not completely match the ambitious but long and carefully planned programme which he had mapped out for himself on his first arrival at Anacapri, when he envisaged that his next six books, along with three already published, would

> form a definite series presenting a more or less complete picture of society in the Midlands before the war. They will be grouped under the name of *The City of Iron* and include: *Undergrowth; Astill's Entire; Abner Fellows; The Young Physician; Lydia* ('The Young Physician 2'); *The Country Doctor; The Seven Sisters; The Iron Age; The Furnace* — the real story of East Africa.
>
> (FBY 781)

Undergrowth, The Iron Age and *The Young Physician* were already published when this plan was formulated. *Abner Fellows* appeared shortly afterwards as *The Black Diamond, The Furnace* was published in 1937 as *They Seek A Country* and *The Country Doctor* in 1938 as *Dr Bradley Remembers*.

In 1923 it was proposed that Francis undertake a lecture tour of America, but this had to be abandoned when he developed appendicitis. Tour notices had already been published, announcing a series of lectures. 'The Romance of Africa' was to deal with the birth of a nation, a subject very dear to Brett Young's heart, but not yet fully matured; 'The Literary Ladder' was to be an estimate of contemporary authors; 'The Form of the Novel' would discuss modern tendencies in fiction; whilst 'The Physician in Literature' would expound the value of a medical education in the making of a novelist.

Eventually in December 1926, with Scott Fitzgerald and his family as fellow-passengers, Francis and Jessie sailed from Naples to New York, where Florence and Tom Lamont, to whom *My Brother Jonathan* would be dedicated, were their hosts. As if designed to welcome the visitors, their arrival in New York coincided with a showing of *Sea*

Horses at a Harlem cinema. The main purpose of the visit was to promote *Portrait of Clare* which Alfred Knopf, who had recently replaced Dutton and Co. as Brett Young's American publishers, had just brought out under the title of *Love Is Enough*.

The four planned topics of 1923 were reduced to two, 'The Confessions of a Novelist' and 'The Doctor in Literature', which Brett Young adeptly expanded to fit the sixteen-lecture programme which his agent J.B. Pond had booked at a variety of academies, colleges, universities, clubs and bookshops. The five-month tour moved north through Connecticut into Massachusetts and west through Pennsylvania and on to Illinois and Wisconsin. A Cotswold journey would later be used to recall the trip through the eyes of a Brett Young character. 'A wide, rolling country it was, not unlike Pennsylvania as he had seen it from a train going westward from Philadelphia' (CB 242). At the National Arts Club in New York, Francis gave advice to aspiring novelists which threw further light on his own understanding of his art.

> What should you write about? Things you know; your home town; autobiography — all novels are. Yet if you lean too heavily on personal experience, imagination atrophies. What ultimately counts is the joy of creation, a passionate desire to give words to dumb emotions clamouring inside.
> (FBY 56)

In addition to the lectures, Francis found time to write an article on Pirandello for the *New York Herald Tribune*, and at the end of the tour he and Jessie enjoyed a trip through the Appalachian and Allegheny Mountains, visiting Washington before sailing for Italy in April 1927.

The next year saw a return visit, this time to promote *My Brother Jonathan*, followed by yet another change in Francis's American publishers, with Alfred Knopf replaced by Harper, in turn destined to be succeeded by Reynal and Hitchcock in 1936. A proposed third American tour in 1933 came to nothing as Brett Young considered the suggested fee to be insufficient.

The few American scenes which found their way into Brett Young's writings suggest that his transatlantic experiences made little impact beyond the commercial. Ludlow Walcot, hero of his own short story, proud of the fact that he had never been east of Long Island or west of Saint Louis, was identified as a caricature of the prototype American businessman with an ulcer, by his clothes and attitudes, both of which were cured by a trip to England. Virginia Murphy, who arrived in Monfalcone as the winner of a scholarship from a Kentucky College of Art and lacked the willpower ever to move on, was stigmatised as much for her nationality as for her apathy. '"I'm not sure she isn't an American," Agnes added, in the precise tone with she might have said; "I'm not sure she isn't a typhoid-carrier"' (MAH 121). Even the American soldiers who, in *The Island* delivered eleventh hour relief to embattled Britain, only returned what the Pilgrim Fathers had carried 'to a stubborn land and a barren shore' (I 228) three hundred years earlier.

When considered in total, despite the reservations of some of his characters, Brett Young's pictures of Capri made up the vision of the earthly paradise sought after by the sixth century Irish saint. 'The crags of Capri swam above the horizon's gentle bow, islanded in the air like the lands of Brendan's vision' (PC 263). It was a paradise also sought by those who adopted the island as their home. In a variety of references to those foreigners who had taken up residence on Capri, Brett Young poked gentle fun at their peculiarities and weaknesses.

> The world of the 'foreign colony' — largely composed of oddities and indifferent dabblers in the Arts, representing a small proportion of chance visitors who, having slipped through the Sirens' talons, remain on the island during the rest of their lives.
> (WL 365-366)

Such 'oddities' and 'indifferent dabblers' generally appeared to have very little choice in the matter. Brett Young first arrived on the Isle of Capri as a matter of economic necessity, and was not ashamed to admit to Hugh Walpole that he remained there for the reason that his books did not earn enough money for him to live comfortably in England. So the exiled members of the lesser English aristocracy who found their way to Capri, were those who were also impoverished, whose wealthier relatives would no longer support them, and who were thus able to stretch small allowances beyond their English purchasing power. There was no other plausible reason for living there that could possibly be conceived by respectable North Bromwich solicitor Ernest Wilburn. 'Pomfret had come a social cropper, for why, otherwise, should he be living in Capri?' (WL 404).

English expatriates who eventually established themselves on the island tended to two extremes of behaviour. There were the moralistic pillars of society, who represented the middle-class values of the community they had left behind, and the artistic who embraced the new freedoms upon which English respectability still frowned. Hugo Pomfret, who but for his desire for privacy would have stood with the second group, met both extremes in the characters of Mrs Robinson and Mrs Spettigue.

> Mrs Spettigue was, by Capri standards, wealthy; the principal pillar of the Anglican Church and guardian of the community's morals.
> (WL 370)

> Mrs Louisa Robinson, was by profession a painter of enormous allegorical pictures composed of nudes so cunningly postured as to avoid giving offence to any eyes but Mrs Spettigue's. Mrs Robinson's villa was the centre of Bohemian life on Capri.
> (WL 372)

The character of Mrs Louisa Robinson obviously relied heavily upon one of the early foreign residents to grace Capri in its emerging Bohemian days — Mrs Sophie Anderson, of the Villa Castello, who had numbered Edwin Cerio's father amongst her pupils and who was famous both for her entertaining and her paintings, which had been exhibited at the Royal Academy since the mid nineteenth century.

It was amongst the genuine oddities and dabblers in the Arts that Francis Brett Young took his place on the island. Native to Capri was Edwin Cerio, whilst established there from abroad were Axel Munthe, the Swedish doctor-author of *The Story of San Michele*, John Ellingham Brooks, lawyer and unsuccessful writer and Compton Mackenzie, remarkable both for his brilliantly coloured clothes: sky-blue tweeds, floral shirts; orange ties; and for his utter and complete devotion to the craft of writing, which Brett Young acknowledged as extraordinary. 'None of the younger men are capable of such sustained flight; we are most of us short story writers gone wrong. Mackenzie seems born to the grand manner' (FBY 1678). Mackenzie's opinion of Brett Young, whom he considered somewhat humourless, was otherwise complimentary, proclaiming him to be an industrious and versatile writer with a romantic outlook on life, whose technical accomplishments showed that he was worthy of much more attention than he had currently received. As assistant to Compton Mackenzie came Eric Brett Young who, in addition to his secretarial duties, worked with Francis adapting Mackenzie's novels *The Vanity Girl* and *Poor Relations* for the stage.

Another long-term, though spasmodic, resident was Norman Douglas, 'physically prepotent, with a clear-cut, pragmatic intelligence and the complete self-assurance of an aristocratic sceptic of the eighteenth century' (FBY 25). Like a character in a Brett Young novel, Douglas arrived on the island penniless and thereafter continually depended upon the generosity of others both to finance his life-style and to shield it from too much public scrutiny. Temporary visitors to the island with whom the Brett Youngs were on visiting terms included Louis Golding, the depressive Jewish poet, writer and temporary journalist, travelling in Italy for health reasons, whom Francis greatly admired. 'I think he is going to be a winner some day' (FBY 889). Archibald Marshall, 'a nice fellow, but too dreadfully restless', (FBY 894) seeking the creative muse, shared an Anacapri villa with Golding, and was a regular visitor to the Villa Fraita, where too came: Charles Morgan, a fledgling writer seeking hospitality; Scott Fitzgerald, with a more than usual penchant for the wine of Capri; Peter Quennell, who wrote four lines each morning and carefully crossed them out each evening; Robert Louis Stevenson's stepson, Lloyd Osborne and the dour but celebrated translator, C.K. Scott-Moncrieff. Such a plethora of artistic genius was almost too much for Brett Young to bear.

> These literary gentlemen are a great responsibility. If we were threatened with a colony of them I should go and live in some Saharan oasis.
> (FBY 894)

Hugh Walpole, renowned for his jealousy of any writer who threatened his reputation, worked on *Wintersmoon* whilst enjoying a holiday with Francis and Jessie. Though appreciating the island's beauty he disliked Capri along with most of its foreign residents, discerning that though the Brett Youngs were undoubtedly kind to needy writers, their rigid high moral stance (compared with the rest of the islanders) also made them unpopular. Walpole's overt homosexuality which caused him to quarrel with Edwin Cerio, also provoked a temporary rift between the enraged Cerio and Brett Young, whom he blamed for concealing Walpole's true nature. Violence threatened when the normally peaceful Francis found himself unable to sleep at night for sorrow at the whole incident and wishing to 'have smashed Cerio's face when he was raving' (FBY 96). Instead he remained silent. Brett Young's private opinion of Walpole suggested a spent talent, an inflated ego and an immodest loquacity.

> Hugh, being dead, contrives to live in letters
> His flatteries have extracted from his betters.
> Hugh loves no woman; yet upon my soul,
> I wish to God he'd practise word-control!
> (FBY 1520)

Following hard on the heels of Francis and Jessie came Frieda and D.H. Lawrence, who appeared a frail little scarecrow of a man with a straggling red beard. With Mackenzie's help, the Lawrences were rapidly established in a fourth floor flat over Morgano's café, from where they equally rapidly passed judgement upon the fawning attendance with which the Brett Youngs waited upon Compton Mackenzie. Though their arrival may have enormously enlivened Capri life, Lawrence shared the view that the island was inhabited by oddities. Brett Young's opinions and judgements proclaimed with all the immodest certainties of a petulant schoolboy, particularly irritated him.

Such views did not inhibit the social life in which the island's literati shared, usually at Mackenzie's home and usually involving recitations, during which Lawrence was easily persuaded to a fulsome rendition of Yeats' 'Lake Isle of Innisfree'; mimicry, at which Mackenzie excelled at making the great appear ludicrous; and music, with Brooks at the piano, Lawrence and Mackenzie joining discordantly in such songs as 'Sally in our Alley' and Francis, who had perfect pitch, looking pained at the whole proceedings. Commonplace though such gatherings may have been, modesty did not intrude. Secker's authors had little doubt that the mantle of English Literature had been placed upon their shoulders, it being no less than their duty to wear it.

> At Solitaria after lunch, I can hear Mackenzie saying: 'It's extraordinary how literary history repeats itself. A hundred

years ago Byron, Shelley and Keats all happened to be living in Italy.' He indicated with a wave of the hand, himself, Lawrence and me. 'You see how well it fits in. Lawrence has been living at Lerici, and you, my dear Francis, like Keats, were once a medical student.'
(MURC — VF 06.1929)

Brett Young had little liking for Frieda, but his feelings regarding Lawrence, who seemed to have lost all impulse to write, were ambivalent. The presence of this 'lovable creature, who is, I think, not quite sane', (FBY 1727) was disturbing, but there was a magnetism about his personality which, despite Lawrence's tendency to repay friendliness with bitterness and to bite the hand that fed him, Francis could not resist. His writing, however, was another matter.

The dreary people who love without restraint and hate without reason are all reincarnations of Lawrence's own pathological soul. As long as he is subject to this demoniacal possession, I don't see any hope for him. It is a pity, for in spite of his sinister influence on myself, I like him immensely.
(FBY 1730)

As it soon became apparent that Capri was too small for so many talents at one time, Lawrence departed for Sicily, Francis and Jessie accompanying him on the hazardous expedition of his search for a new home. *The Red Knight* set in the Mediterranean Republic of Trinacria, owed much of its atmosphere to Lawrence and to Sicily.

It is certainly written more elaborately than any of my earlier books and I can only attribute this change to the Sicilian adventure in Lawrence's stimulating company.
(RK Preface)

Shortly before he died, Lawrence finally and scathingly dismissed the talents of Brett Young, whose public recognition was growing by the day, as 'puny'. Francis's final public comment upon the writer whose fame would far outshine his own, revealed no resentment at the way in which Lawrence had used but scorned him, only admiration for work which had been achieved in spite of demons.

Poor, tormented Lawrence,
That frail, hag-ridden Titan, whose abhorrence

Of Reason, frothed with ineffectual rage,
Flaws the pure crystal of a lyric page
Unmatched in power or beauty since he died.
(I 437)

In private, however, approbation was balanced by censure.

Lawrence could write; yet why should I believe
In one who wears his privates on his sleeve?
(FBY 1520)

Despite their public mutual admiration, and the fact that the
principal players in this island drama may have had great reservations about each other, there was, amongst these adoptive Capresi,
the practice of open house and open-handed generosity such as that
which the Brett Youngs received from Compton Mackenzie; Drogo
D'Abitot from Mr Potts and John Ellingham Brooks from Brett
Young. The ties which bound them were those of Art, penury and
the search for public recognition.

As Brett Young's fame and fortune increased, the amount of time
spent on Capri decreased. During the 1930s, visits to Fraita were no
longer included in the annual programme. This was not entirely due
to the author's increased funds, but also to the political situation in
Italy. The easy-going atmosphere of Capri had been seriously
impaired by Mussolini's rise to power, which led first to Brett Young
staying away from his erstwhile island paradise, love of his native
land overriding that of Italy, whose press was being actively encouraged to vilify England; then to his inclusion amongst those foreign
nationals required to pay forced loans on their Italian property; and
finally to the sequestration of Villa Fraita. When the war was over,
Brett Young experienced some difficulty in reclaiming his Capri
property, and sought the assistance of the Foreign Office.

When the property was sequestrated at the beginning of the
war it was roughly treated and the land was let to a rabid
Fascist who thought it proper to exploit it through hatred of
the English. I do not know what that means, but guess that it
may be that he has cut down olive trees and other plantations
of fruit. My wife, as owner of the property, would like to
appoint Edwin Cerio of Capri as her agent.
(FBY 1853)

After an absence of some years, Francis and Jessie returned briefly to Capri in 1949 to arrange for the disposal of their moveable property, and the sale of Villa Fraita, for three thousand five hundred pounds, to Ian Greenlees, Head of the British Council in Rome. Though, before leaving for the last time, Francis donated a quantity of books from his collection to Edwin Cerio and to the English Library in Capri, his final comment showed that he was out of humour with the island paradise which had been the scene of so much creative talent.

> The island has sadly changed. First an American occupation and now occupation by hordes of the Industrial Norths of Italy and England have made it hardly recognisable as the Arcadian island which we loved. Pansies, tourists of the cheaper sort and Gracie Fields have pretty well finished it off between them.
>
> (FBY 3478)

Eight: Recognition

Prolonged residence in Capri with comparatively short visits to England persuaded Francis Brett Young that he was losing touch with his native land. This anxiety, coupled with improving health, suggested that the time was right to return home. Strangely it was not in Devon, where he had practised medicine, nor in the border-lands with which he had a self-confessed affinity, nor yet in his enchanted Worcestershire that he chose to live. A remembered holiday with Jessie, accompanied by Gertrude Dale as requisite chaperon, in Hawkshead in 1907, and his Lakeland honeymoon at Skelwith Bridge, convinced Francis of his desire to live near Esthwaite Water. Returning from a visit to Hugh Walpole's Brackenburn estate in Borrowdale, Francis and Jessie discovered an unoccupied Georgian house some two miles south of Hawkshead. 'Esthwaite Lodge', built above the lake at the beginning of the nineteenth century, was purchased at the beginning of the twentieth, by the family of Liverpool shipping magnates, Thomas and John Brocklebank, who leased the property to a series of tenants.

Francis and Jessie moved into Esthwaite Lodge in July 1929, employing, in contrast to the simple life of Anacapri, a chauffeur, a housemaid and two gardeners. Here Francis would write three of his major Mercian novels: *Jim Redlake*, *Mr and Mrs Pennington* and *The House Under The Water*. Though the Lake District featured hardly at all in his writing, its majesty was of that same unblighted quality which so appealed to him in his own beloved borderlands.

> A green immaculate Eden, undefiled
> By fallen man's devices — where the wild
> Valleys and fells of Cumberland condense
> In compass small more beauties than the sense
> Or mind may measure.
> (I 384-385)

A regular visitor who admired Brett Young's new home was Hugh Walpole. The writing room which he commissioned above his library at Brackenburn was inspired by the bedroom at Esthwaite Lodge in which part of *Judith Paris* was written. Among other visitors were Edward Marsh, William Armstrong and Florence Hardy, though the nearby River Kent offered escape even from such engaging society. Here, smoking a pipe of his favourite Magaliesberg tobacco, Francis wiled away the hours in the delights to which Owen Lucton was introduced.

> All the fisherman heard was the sweetest, the most enchant-ing of sounds: the noise of running water amid surroundings that were far from the haunts of men. If one were tired, or the fish wouldn't take a fly, one could sit on the bank and smoke a reflective pipe and watch the life of the river.
> (MLF 315)

Esthwaite however proved less ideal than Brett Young had antici-pated. Spiritually, it did not meet his yearning for his native soil; geographically, it was remote from Heinemann, London and the Midlands. Following a collision involving another car at a crossroads, during a chauffeur-driven journey from Esthwaite to Birmingham, Brett Young suffered from severe shock and cracked ribs. In the seconds immediately before their motor accidents, Owen Lucton, Ludlow Walcot and Jack Ombersley each vividly relived the horror of Brett Young's own crash, in reactions that could only have come from personal experience.

Instinctively Mr Lucton knew that he had lost control of his car.

> Though he tried to right it, it would not obey him. He was swerving to the left in a front-wheel skid that he could not correct: at the mercy of two tons of metal hurled sideways through space.
> (MLF 74)

Mr Walcot was aware of nothing but on-coming headlights.

> Another car was coming towards him, whirling madly down-hill. It filled all the narrow lane with its light and the roar of its engine.
> (CB 247)

Unforgettable sounds and smells filled Jack Ombersley's consciousness.

There was a screech of dry rubber tearing, a smell of rubber burning. A tyre burst with the sound of a gun-shot, but that sound was drowned in the crash of the great car hurtling into a telegraph-pole, the splinter of glass.
(TLW 525)

Distressing though Brett Young's accident undoubtedly was, it became yet another episode to be added to the bank of experiences upon which he would draw for future novels.

Following the success of *Mr and Mrs Pennington*, Francis at last felt able to invest some of his hard-earned literary income in his beloved Worcestershire. His banker-friend Robert Holland-Martin took him to see a neglected house near Pershore, the possibilities of which were not only immediately recognised — 'surely in its own style and size one of the most beautiful examples of eighteenth century domestic architecture in England, delightful not only in its proportions, material and workmanship, but also in the grace and restraint of the decorations' (FBY 41) — but captured in 'Enemy Alien', a short story in which Leon Bernstein impulsively purchased Chadcombe near Fladbourne, thirty-two acres and 'a rectangular Adam house of warm yellow stone with beautifully proportioned windows, a fanlight door, and classic urns adorning the corner of its moulded cornice' (CHo 41).

Designed (according to Pevsner, though Brett Young was less categorical) by George Byfield and built overlooking the Avon near Fladbury by George Perrott in 1791, the Adam-style Craycombe House with thirty-seven acres which Brett Young bought from G.H. Cuming Butler in June 1932, derived its name from its parkland rookery or 'crows' combe'. A similar feature marked Chaddesbourne Hall. 'Elms shadowed the Hall. "I'm glad there's a rookery here," Helen Ombersley thought. "No Worcestershire house would feel right without its rookery."' (TLW 41).

For several months Francis and Jessie travelled from Esthwaite to supervise restoration work at Craycombe. Overgrown trees which shadowed the house were felled. Woodmen from the Holland-Martin's Overbury estate came to remove a monster sequoia, reputedly the tallest in the West Midlands, leaving a twenty yard crater after winching out its roots. Chaddesbourne Hall again was the setting for a fictional recreation.

The felling of the great sequoia, indeed, was a job! Before the

axes would bite, a six-inch felting of fibre must be stripped
from the trunk. When it leaned and crashed, like a falling
church spire, the whole building shook and light flooded the
house like a sudden burst of sunshine.

(TLW 128)

The architect Guy Dawber was commissioned to restore Craycombe House to its original design, demolishing the various exten-
sions added by previous occupants. Removal of paint, dark
chocolate from the woodwork and canary yellow from the walls,
revealed unexpected treasures. The three pears of the Perrott arms,
which decorated the marble mantelpiece of the afternoon room,
were curiously reminiscent of the three Worcestershire pears with
which Heinemann had embellished the cover of *Portrait of Clare* in
1927, and which would invariably be used on their subsequent
editions of Brett Young's works. The nine muses were discovered
moulded in gesso on the pinewood mantelpiece of the library, where
the frieze displayed a selection of poets and philosophers, and the
cornice, Roman emperors. Similar dramatic effects of restoration at
Chaddesbourne Hall were witnessed by Dr Selby.

> The dull tinge, which formerly absorbed every glimmer of
> light, had been banished from the walls, revealing an unsus-
> pected wealth of plaster-work, that, freed from successive
> incrustations of paint, now displayed the formal delicacy of a
> Georgian craftsman's hand in swags, medallions and fluent
> traceries.
>
> (TLW 120-121)

In December 1932, the Brett Youngs' furniture was delivered from
Esthwaite Lodge, accompanied by Chauffeur Little, who would live
in the flat over the stables. There, scratched on windows and walls,
Francis read the names of prisoners-of-war, Karl Fleisch and Hans
Muller, which, with their defiant 'Deutschland uber alles!', gave him
an idea for 'Enemy Alien', in which, like Craycombe, Chadcombe
was used as a First World War prison camp.

> The surface of the door at the end of the loft was scribbled
> with chalk in a Gothic script. There were several signatures:
> Karl Fleisch, Hans Muller, Georg Pfeifer, and a triumphant
> scroll that read 'Deutschland uber Alles!'.
>
> (CHo 45)

Joining forces with the Craycombe gardeners, Collins, Salisbury and Shelton (who gave his name to the gamekeeper in *White Ladies*, a novel written at Craycombe House), Harry Little formed a handbell ringing team for the entertainment of Brett Young's guests. In Monk's Norton, Francis established a similar group.

> A team of handbell-ringers ring changes — Plain and Treble Bobs and Grandsire Triples and Stedmans and complicated Surprises — to the tune of ten thousand on their silvery, singing chime.
> (PV 167)

In the same group of servants, Brett Young found the nucleus of a cricket eleven which he recreated in Harry Kington, Jim Perkins and other villagers whom Owen Lucton met when conscripted to the local team by the angling parson at Hay-on-Wye. In addition to gardeners and chauffeur, Craycombe Wanderers included the local butcher, a railway porter, various Fladbury villagers and, occasionally, such distinguished visitors as novelists C.P. Snow and Harry Hoff, Jock Finlay, the South African rugby referee and Charles Lyttelton, Worcestershire County's cricket captain.

To complete the staff came Marietta Massimino, whom Francis and Jessie brought from Anacapri to be maid at Craycombe, and cook-housekeeper Vera Lewis, who found the household the happiest in which she ever worked. Each, however, occupied a known place in the social hierarchy. The motto which Brett Young placed on the frieze at The Moat at Chaddesbourne was a statement of his own convictions.

> WHYLE : EVERY : MAN : IS : PLESED : IN : HIS : DEGRE :
> THERE : IS : BOTH : PEASE : AND : UNETI.
> (TLW 161)

After lunch at the Malvern home of Canadian novelist Mazo de la Roche, Francis and Jessie once returned to Craycombe earlier than expected, and were upset to find their domestic staff relaxing in deck chairs on the lawn. Mr Lucton's unexpected return to Alvaston Grange discovered Fowler, the butler, 'in shirt-sleeves sitting in a deck-chair smoking a cigar and luxuriously contemplating the second gardener at work' (MLF 452).

At Craycombe, when they were not mixing with the county set

(Baldwins, Cobhams, Holland-Martins, Mary Anderson de Navarro), or attending the Worcestershire Hunt Ball, or receiving visitors (Mr and Mrs Bernard Shaw, Mr and Mrs Robert Dolbey, Lloyd George and Frances Stevenson, Hugh Walpole, Gwen Ffrangcon-Davies), the Brett Youngs adopted a simple life-style. Each morning at eleven, Francis would take his daily drink of powdered sanatogen served in milk. Midday lunch invariably concluded with fruitcake and cheese. Italian recipes were popular for evening meals, especially macaroni, made by Vera and dried over the back of a chair in the garden, and gnocchi, a base of eggs, milk and ground rice, covered in Parmesan cheese. Dessert frequently consisted of bottled plums from Craycombe's own orchards. Waste was abhorred: to avoid the cost of dog biscuits, Vera's home-made bread, when stale, was baked hard for Bailey, Francis's ill-tempered Bedlington terrier.

Arrival at Craycombe stimulated a series of novels with a Worcestershire setting, the first of which was actually begun aboard the world's largest warship, *HMS Hood*. Concerned with the desirability of enhancing its public reputation at a time when the danger of German rearmament was obvious, in 1933 the Royal Navy invited four well-known writers to join the autumn manoeuvres of the Battle Cruiser Squadron. The object of this exercise was that unquestionably reliable and patriotic authors would write about naval life from first-hand experience. Brett Young's involvement in, and account of, the Tanga campaign, made him an obvious choice. H.M. Tomlinson, the novelist and travel-writer, had already focused on things maritime and had been a war correspondent in Belgium and France. Chairman of Methuen & Co., E.V. Lucas, who had been made a Companion of Honour in the previous year, had established his reputation as an authority on Charles Lamb, but also wrote prolifically in a whole range of genres. A.P. Herbert, of *Misleading Cases* fame, had been mentioned in despatches at Gallipoli, was on the staff of *Punch* magazine and would bring a lighter touch to the project.

For his part in this programme, Francis boarded *HMS Hood* at Invergordon in October. As a direct result of the voyage which followed, *This Little World* was dedicated to Vice Admiral James of the Battle-Cruiser Squadron, 'partly because the first words of it were written in your cabin in those delightful days when we rounded Cape Wrath' (TLW Dedication). Otherwise the cruise made little obvious impact upon Brett Young's writing. Indeed, his comments when the *Hood* was sunk off Greenland by the *Bismarck* in

1941, suggest that he thought of the voyage as a vacation.

> I was saddened beyond words by the loss of the Hood in which I spent a delightful holiday with Bubbles James in 1933. She was a lovely ship.
> (FBY 3076)

On his new Craycombe estate, Brett Young entered enthusiastically into the role of market gardener and farmer, raising pigs and sheep and growing fruit. From these personal experiences came many of the agricultural scenes in *Portrait of a Village*, the book written in just thirty-eight days of 1936, partly as a vehicle for the wood-engravings which Heinemann (at the instigation of Edward Marsh) had commissioned from the young Joan Hassall. Though the outcome was a gem of both text and illustration, the collaboration was not particularly happy. Hassall found Francis an over-critical colleague, and was intimidated by Jessie's constant name-dropping and social pretensions (the very character flaws which caused the Capri islanders to find her uncongenial) and the insistence of them both that he be addressed as Major. Francis, in his turn, was frustrated by Joan's apparent tardiness, writing impatiently to Charles Evans, his Heinemann publisher: 'I hope you are keeping an eye on Joan Hassall. She is the kind of creature who would hang anybody's book up for years if she had her own way' (FBY 1526). In fact the book was delayed and the serial rights of *Portrait of a Village* were sold to *Good Housekeeping*, which published the story, illustrated by Rowland Hillder, before the appearance of Heinemann's edition. Brett Young's irritation with Joan Hassall over this delay was obviously never forgotten, as thirteen years later, when corresponding with A.S. Frere at Heinemann over the possibility of a new edition of the book, he commented: 'I agree with you that Joan Hassall's illustrations are quite unimportant' (FBY 1594).

The Wessex Saddleback pigs and Kerry Hill sheep reared at Craycombe, though initially delightful, were not cheap, as Mr Rudge discovered at Monk's Norton.

> By the time he had finished stocking with Wessex Saddleback pigs and Kerry Hill sheep and replanted half of the orchard with Victoria plums and Cox's apples, he had made a big hole in his dwindling capital.
> (PV 107)

In a description of the healthy and profitable flock of sheep belonging to Mr Rudge's neighbour, Brett Young slipped easily into the appropriate technical vocabulary of farming.

> Mr Collins believes in latish yeaning, when the keep gets more growth in it. He crosses the Kerry Hill ewe with the Suffolk ram, and their offspring combine the nimbleness of their dams with the sire's sturdy build. Mr Collins' ewes show no maggot-eaten patches of their fleece, nor limping foot-rot.
> (PV 120)

Unfortunately the Craycombe Kerry Hills did suffer from foot-rot and the flock was sold, Francis himself adopting the very policy upon which he had Mr Rudge decide, namely to 're-plant all that's left of the orchard and break up the rest of the land gradually for plums' (PV 110).

In the Craycombe orchards Brett Young planted one thousand new fruit trees, much of the produce of which, along with potatoes, beans, peas and red currants also grown in the thirty-five acres under cultivation, was sold at Pershore market. Though employing extra help at harvest time, particularly during the war years when Italian prisoners served as fruit-pickers, Francis was very much a 'hands-on' owner, who used the labours of the field as a diversion from those of the study, and who was conversant with market economy and the mercurial price of plums.

> When there are plenty they sell for as little as one-and-six-pence a pot of seventy-two pounds: when they sell for twenty-four shillings a pot they are usually so scarce that it makes little difference. If there is a glut, the canners and bottlers beat you down. If they are scarce they do the same, having canned or bottled all they need in the last year of plenty.
> (PV 112)

Brett Young's arrival at Craycombe was closely followed by a mark of recognition which undoubtedly gladdened his heart: the first volumes of a new edition of his works. Between 1934 and 1956 twenty-seven books appeared in the popular Severn Edition. Initially modestly priced at five shillings, Francis appraised the series in terms that were anything but modest. 'I like the Severn format very much. It should make an attractive line of books and be indispensable to every middle-class bookshelf in four counties' (FBY 1521).

Despite the pleasure of Craycombe, Worcestershire winters remained more than Francis's health could endure and some substitute, both climatic and creative, for Anacapri was obviously needed. On the south coast of Cornwall, between Looe and Polperro, he discovered a cottage, reminiscent of Fraita, standing high on the cliffs of Talland Bay. Here, in 1936, he invested the latest profits of his writing. A short walk from The Cobbles, where some of Walpole's early books were written, the house looked out towards the Eddystone Lighthouse across 'oceans's running surges, the fury that beats / On iron-bound cliffs of Cornwall' (I 6). The mild Cornish climate as a winter retreat made life in Worcestershire possible for the remainder of each year, until a permanent and complete change eventually became unavoidable.

As he received the dedications of other writers' works (Louis Golding's *Magnolia Street*, Compton Mackenzie's *Literature in my Time*, John Moore's *Country Men*), the Craycombe years brought the recognition which Brett Young desired. He became a valued presence on various fund-raising platforms and had his name added to the councils of numerous official bodies, all further grist to the inspirational mill for current writing; encounters which, simply because they were part of his own life-experience, commanded a place, however transitory, in his imaginary world.

> Books written in the transport of joy and tenderness that arose from my return, after twenty-five years of distant exile, to the county in which I was born and to the scenes of my childhood.
> (TLW Preface ix)

Within these childhood scenes, Francis joined the Worcestershire Archaeological Society, became a member of the Council of the Worcestershire Historical Society and was elected a vice president of the Worcestershire Association, an organisation, with Stanley Baldwin as President, established to foster a love of the county. For this Brett Young's own credentials, expressed in distant South Africa by young Richard Abberley, were impeccable.

> Worcestershire is the most perfect place in the world; it's the centre of my life and dreams; it's what I care most about. It's right in the middle of England; you couldn't get nearer its heart if you tried.
> (CG 273)

The first garden party which Francis and Jessie hosted at Craycombe was attended by over one hundred members of the Worcestershire Association. After tea on the lawn, the house was opened for the visitors, and though the weather was fine and the garden colourful, the stress of the occasion was more than the hosts could endure, and their first garden party was also their last.

Worcestershire County Cricket Club, avidly followed by Francis, of which he also became a vice president, was one of the talking-points of Monk's Norton.

> When Worcestershire, on a crumbling wicket at Kidderminster, beat Yorkshire by eleven runs, the whole village was instantly abuzz with triumphant delight. Reg Perks, 'Doc' Gibbons, Cyril Walters, Dick Howorth and 'the Honourable Charles', were names as familiar as if they were boon-companions.
> (PV 145)

A member of the Executive Committee of the Friends of Worcester Cathedral, Brett Young expressed something of his affection for the building through Dr Selby of Chaddesbourne D'Abitot.

> He had always loved it; it was *the* cathedral to him; a graceful, mediaeval lady of a church compared with round-headed Norman warriors like Durham and York.
> (TLW 592) ·

It was not only to Worcester Cathedral that Brett Young gave his support. Answering an appeal from John Moore for the restoration of Tewkesbury Abbey Tower, he joined with Bernard Shaw and John Masefield in an outdoor meeting held where one of *The Island's* three rivers would sing its song: 'The wide, flood-whitened fields that lie / Beneath the tower of Tewkesbury' (I 122-123). Subsequently Francis became a member of the Council of the Friends of Tewkesbury Abbey. Unlike Mr Lucton, who spotted the distant tower of Pershore but had no time to look at it, he also found time to address the Annual Meeting of the Friends of Pershore Abbey. Along with that of Evesham Abbey, these two towers marked out the heart of Brett Young's little world.

> Wherever the geographical centre of England may be, the spiritual centre is somewhere in the neighbourhood of the confluence of Severn and Avon, where the three great abbey

towers of Evesham, Pershore and Tewkesbury rise from the base of Bredon Hill.
(FBY 55)

The boyhood walks which Francis enjoyed in Worcestershire and the Welsh borderlands found their public recognition in his appointment as President of the Midland Federation of the Ramblers' Association, an organisation at which he poked gentle fun through Bert Hopkins of Wednesford.

'It's a fine show, our Association and if ever you thought of taking up rambling seriously — we don't want any triflers mind! — you ought to belong to it. Reduced railway fares, the loan of maps, and full lists of decent accommodation where a chap can be sure he's not going to be rooked for his B. and B. All for half a dollar a year.'
(MLF 180-181)

As his public recognition increased, Brett Young was called upon to present the prizes and to address the Faculty of Medicine at the University of Birmingham where, like himself, Edwin Ingleby and Jonathan Dakers had already studied and where John Bradley was still to go. In support of Queen's Hospital, one of the University's teaching establishments, Craycombe House was opened to the public and a commemorative leaflet printed. When a new wing was completed at Birmingham Throat Hospital, it was Brett Young who was invited to perform the opening ceremony. At the invitation of the Royal Society of Literature (whose offer of a fee-paying rather than honorary membership he petulantly declined) Francis read a paper entitled 'The Doctor in Literature' in which he established a primary source of inspiration.

Not in those centres where art is in the air — Chelsea or Montmartre, or even Bloomsbury — but places where life and death are in the air; in other words the general hospitals of our great cities.
(DL - EDH 20)

After Francis became President of the newly-formed Cheltenham Literary Society, it was not surprising that its Secretary, Cecil Day Lewis, should merit a passing reference in a Brett Young novel, in which the author gave his opinion of poets past and present through

Diana Powys's assessment of her friend Alistair Shiel. 'He isn't recognised as a major poet, like Shelley or Auden or Milton or Cecil Day Lewis' (MLF 284). Nor was it surprising that Brett Young should have been elected first Vice Chairman of the Worcestershire Branch of the Council for the Preservation of Rural England, sharing as he did the conviction of many poets, that if God had made the country-side then man had despoiled it by building towns. John Bradley became yet another expression of his creator's dogmas.

> His countryman's soul rebelled against those sad culverts lined by endless red-brick rows and blue-brick pavements down which the human tide ebbed and flowed like ordure swinging in an estuary.
> (DBR 295-296)

Taking up the countryman's mantle in a series of letters to *The Times*, Brett Young deprecated the damage that would befall the Malvern Hills if a proposed extension to existing quarrying were permitted. Apart from geographical and environmental spoliation, there was the aesthetic claim to consider.

> These hills are sacred soil in the history of English Literature. From their slopes William Langland saw the 'Fields full of Folk' in the 'Vision of Piers Plowman'. In their shadow the genius of Elizabeth Barrett was nursed. In our own time their shapes have dominated the youthful imagination of such artists as Housman, Masefield, Galsworthy and Elgar.
> (T 16.10.1937)

While Francis balanced the roles of author and country squire, Jessie ensured an efficient household, as she busied herself in the supervision of the laundry and the weekly grocery orders, which, on the occasions when she did not deal directly with Fortnum and Mason, came from stores in Worcester. Village traders were ignored, perhaps because they resembled Mr Cantlow in Monk's Norton.

> There is hardly anything essential to life in the country that cannot be raked up from the recesses of Mr Cantlow's shop: he prides himself on the comprehensiveness of his stock, though there is also nothing that cannot be bought at least ten per cent cheaper and better in Worcester.
> (PV 31)

It was Jessie who signed the cheques and paid the bills. The flowers which decorated each room, including those of the servants, were arranged by her. Her whole purpose in life was to protect the Major from the exigencies of daily routine and to provide a peaceful and ordered structure in which he might work undisturbed, all else being subservient to his needs. Ill-health still plagued him: the black curtains in his dressing-room were to soothe his migraines. Work still possessed him: Craycombe servants were ignored simply because he did not notice them when the lyrical muse gripped him. As at Brixham Jessie had guarded him from the assaults of the telephone and the surgery bell so she continued to raise a cordon of veneration around him at Craycombe. Her vigilance admitted no exceptions: not the village children playing noisily with their wheelbarrows under his window, whom she banished to a distant field; not Fladbury's fund-raising choirmaster, Charlie Clemens, who could not be admitted as Francis had an inspiration; not Hugh Walpole whom she would not allow outside the study door, lest Francis be disturbed.

In Jessie's eyes, the sanctity of her husband's person obviously extended to his possessions. When Charles Evans admired a pair of stockings which Jessie had knitted for Francis to wear with his plus-fours, she offered to knit him a pair too. Some time passed before Evans received a note from Jessie apologising that she had not had time to knit the stockings, but enclosing instead the heavily-darned pair which Francis wore whilst writing *Dr Bradley Remembers*.

This cocoon of adoration in which Jessie wrapped Francis un-doubtedly fed his ego and blunted his self-critical faculty. In her eyes everything that he wrote was beyond criticism and the orbit of all lesser mortals eclipsed by his light. There is but a fine divide between cosseting and stifling and Jessie must often have crossed it.

Following Francis's death, Jessie, who at some point in her hus-band's rise to fame had changed her public name to Jessica, entered into agreement with Arnold Gyde that, based on material which she would supply, he would write Francis's biography. From the outset it was evident that she wished to feature more prominently, both in the writing and in the finished narrative, than Gyde planned. With some prudence, he attempted to ease the situation, explaining that his aim was to present her as the most helpful wife that an English author of the twentieth century had, a task which would have been neither modest nor tactful for Jessie to attempt herself. Despite advice from her intended literary executor C.P. Snow (whose caricature of her appeared in *Corridors of Power* as Mrs Henneker, persistently pestering Lewis Eliot to read passages from her biographical eulogy of her late husband) Jessie insisted that the initial agreement be amended to credit her and Gyde with joint authorship. Continued interference and cavilling notes reminding her partner that for every two hours that he worked on the biography, she worked for seven or eight, made the outcome inevitable. Gyde wrote to her of the embryonic biography that as it seemed increasingly like a book about Jessie by Jessie, he could not assent to his name being associated with it. Reluctantly and self-righteously, Jessie agreed to pay him one hundred and fifty pounds compensation for the work which he had already done, on the understanding that he had no further involvement with the project.

Jessie's re-written, pretentious and adulatory account of Francis's life, which fading memory rendered less than error-free, exhausted superlatives in assessing his succeeding works as each more perfect than its predecessor. That the book would inevitably devote much space to its writer could perhaps have been foretold by South African novelist Jillian Becker, whose teenage question to Francis concerning the date of one of his books brought the withering answer from Jessie that none of Francis's important books had been written before he married her. After considerable editing of the lengthy manuscript and rejection by several publishers, Jessie's biography was eventually published, partly at her own expense, by Heinemann in 1962.

Francis's devotion to Jessie was, however, as absolute as hers to him. The idealism of their courting days never faded, and his hopes of 1906 remained true throughout their life together. 'The word "wife" suggests to me a high sanctity — an infinite peace. At the same time it carries with it a caress of great tenderness' (FBY 191). Theirs was a real love-match, in which the two of them lived very much unto themselves, the domestic staff never hearing raised voices between them, because there never were raised voices. They were indeed a couple who lived happily ever after, as Francis's dedication of *The Island* to Jessie made absolutely plain.

> Dearest, in all my life I have known but two
> Unwavering loves: for England and for you.

The idea for an epic presentation of English history was a long-standing dream of Brett Young's, first conceived in the early 1920s, when a few lines eventually to be incorporated into *The Island's* 'Invocation' were written. Antecedents prior even to that may be traced, as 'Song of the Dark Ages', the poem with which *Five Degrees South* opened, was reworked as 'The Trench Diggers: Salisbury Plain' for *The Island*, the composition of which began in 1939.

> In days when the very existence of Britain was imperilled, the writing of anything so flimsy as fiction seemed out of tune with the times. I resumed the discarded project of trying to give shape in verse to my thoughts and feeling about my native land.
> (I vi, Foreword: Limited Edition)

Just as Brett Young had been a poet of the First World War, who expressed himself in prose during the years of peace, so the outbreak of the Second World War recalled him to what was, perhaps, his most natural genre, unsparing though the task would be.

> The Muse does not smile on a neglectful lover; my ear had been attuned too long to the rhythms of prose and conformed with difficulty to the more stringent discipline of verse.
> (I vi, Foreword: Limited Edition)

Discipline in writing however was not alien to Brett Young's nature, and the composition of *The Island* exhausted his already failing strength, as he became thoroughly absorbed in the writing of this history,

> designed to show the continuity of life in this island from geological times. It would be my 'Dynasts' though the protagonists would not be the great figures of our history, but the humbler folk who live against that background of events.
> (FBY 1541)

So a retired Roman centurion reminisced to a young subaltern on the slopes of Bredon Hill about the state of Britain in 78 A.D.; a dying Worcester monk chronicled de Montfort's achievements; the Civil War was refought in the memory of Bill Shelton, taverner of Worcester. Repeating the unity favoured for the novels, Worcestershire and the borderlands provided the backcloth against which the common man observed and commented upon the events which shaped Brett

Young's world: a world in which the beauties of England, its flowers, birds and rivers, as well as its history, might be sung.

An impressive diversity of literary construction, dramatic, narrative and lyrical was utilized. Verses ranged through couplets and quatrains to produce both ballads and irregular stanzas; lines most usually written in pentameter, where more appropriate employed tetrameter or octosyllables, heptameter or fourteeners; metre incorporated anapest, trochee and spondee; sections were introduced and scenes set by passages of prose; Roman and italic type counterpoised words, phrases and entire stanzas. Brett Young sought accuracy in content and exactness in expression. In this he was helped by the encouragement and advice of a number of friends including St John Ervine, Charles Evans and C.P. Snow.

Since the publication of *The Tragic Bride* in 1920, however, Brett Young had particularly benefited from the skilful proofreading of his friend and admirer Edward Marsh, to whom he dedicated *White Ladies*, and with whom he enjoyed a regular correspondence detailing the joys and sorrows of his latest creations. Marsh, editor of *Georgian Poetry*, patron of the arts and private secretary to Winston Churchill, had evolved a highly critical and censorious discipline of proofreading, appropriately called 'diabolization', which he also exercised on behalf of a number of other writers, including Churchill, Walpole and Somerset Maugham, in whose works Francis detected signs of tribulation.

> Maugham is a most interesting writer, his characters so minutely observed and detailed. They would come to life if he'd let them, but I think he has a horror of anything so uncontrolled as an act of creation. This man must have suffered more than most.
> (FBY 1538)

Marsh scrutinised the text of *The Island* with the same vigilance and attention to detail with which Brett Young wrote it. In the original draft of 'The Tale of Aedwulf the Dispossessed' (a poem which used words of only Anglo-Saxon origin) the narrator looked upon the fallen King Harold.

> As I gazed at him
> With eyes distraught, a lance-point ripped my flank
> And flung me flat and senseless, where I lay

Sprawling amid the dead...
    (I 99)

Marsh's recognition that 'ripped my flank' was a repetition of an identical wound three pages earlier, brought a change to 'ripped my ribs' in the published version. Punctuation received the same thorough investigation. In 'Songs of the Three Rivers', Brett Young wrote:

When fierce imagination fell
To burn upon the prosy page —
And the wide skies became a stage...
    (I 120)

Marsh replaced the dash with a comma and recommended the substitution of 'till' for 'and', both of which changes Brett Young accepted. In 'The Tale of John De Mathon', it was the effect of faulty pronunciation upon metre that attracted Marsh's censure.

Earl Simon's friends forsook him: Gloucester and Norfolk,
Bohun and Mortimer and Roger Bigod
Who had been freedom's spokesmen — all forsook him.
    (I 133)

The published version made the change which to Edward Marsh was glaringly obvious. As 'Bohun' was actually pronounced 'Boon', to write 'And Bohun' would supply the missing beat.

Immediate recognition followed the publication of *The Island* with 27,500 copies sold in the first week. The following September brought further recognition when 'The Winged Victory' was quoted in Liverpool Cathedral at a service to commemorate the Battle of Britain. Francis Brett Young himself was in no doubt that *The Island* was his crowning achievement and that it was in poetry that his heart and mind together spoke the words by which he would choose to be remembered.

I have tried to write prose which conformed to my own
conceptions of what is beautiful. Even so, I think the best of
me is to be found in my long epic poem 'The Island'.
    (FBY 1108)

At the outbreak of war, Craycombe had been prepared to receive evacuees. In fact members of staff from the BBC radio station at

Wood Norton, including playwright and producer, Lance Sieveking, whom Francis had first met in General Smuts' army, were billeted there. In 1940 the Adam fireplaces and friezes were boarded up when the house was handed over to the Red Cross as a soldiers' convalescent hospital. Now the Brett Youngs' time was divided between reduced accommodation at Talland (which had also been requisitioned for evacuees) where Francis became chairman of Looe Civil Defence Committee, and Craycombe, where they occupied the orangery (turning part of it into a music room) and the gardener's cottage (where a bedroom became a writing room). Francis's frustration at the Ministry of Information's rejection of his offer to liaise between South Africa and Rhodesia was obvious.

> It appears to me ridiculous that men like myself and Priestley, among the leaders of our profession, should be excluded from performing the work which we are best qualified to do.
> (FBY 1530)

A renewed public interest in his earlier writing might well, it seemed to Francis, be a by-product of war, in which his readers would recognise 'the virtues of the long Midland novels as satisfying reading, in price and in bulk, for black-out evenings; also their representative Englishness' (FBY 1531). 'Englishness', always important to Brett Young, was particularly so in time of war. Nowhere did he express this more forcibly than in his opinion of P.G. Wodehouse who, on the German occupation of France, had been taken from his home in Le Touquet to Berlin, from where he broadcast to America.

> I have always resented that fellow Wodehouse dodging his income-tax, but this purchase of freedom at the price of pandering to the Nazis goes beyond that. I don't know the man. He may be God's own charmer socially, but politically he is contemptible; unfit for the society of decent Englishmen.
> (FBY 1549)

Though his years at Esthwaite, Craycombe and Talland had undoubtedly brought recognition to Francis Brett Young, they also marked his increasing awareness of Hamlet's sorrowful conclusion that the time was out of joint. When his own name did not appear in a list of possible future literary giants in a competition organised by the *Daily Mail* in February 1933, Francis bristled with righteous indignation, that he,

> one of the pieces de resistance of Heinemann's list; an author with twenty not negligible novels to his name, including a number that have sold over 25,000 copies, should not even be included as a possible!
>
> (FBY 1519)

Awareness that other writers were recognised whilst he was over-looked provoked Francis to a cynical and vitriolic consideration of how he might have sought similar popularity for *This Little World*.

> I should have made Colonel Ombersley the victim of an Oedipus complex, his son and daughter homosexual, George Cookson a sadist, Mrs Ombersley a suppressed nympho-maniac, Aaron Bunt an addict to bestiality and the parson to self-abuse. If all these characters had been mixed up in a welter of mud, lust and mysticism, I should have achieved a novel worthy of being compared with the Herries Chronicle.
>
> (FBY 1521)

This, however, was not the style of Brett Young who, because he wrote penetratingly but never salaciously, with a doctor's observa-tion and poet's gift for words, would inevitably not be complacent when assessing his life's work with absolute honestly.

> I have written twenty novels, goodish, bad and indifferent, and the hell of it is that I cannot feel any real satisfaction in the results of my struggle up the slopes of Helicon.
>
> (FBY 2145)

Of the four projects which Francis hoped to complete during these years (*Chadminster*, a story of a Mercian cathedral city and its inhabitants; a romantic novel set in Capri during the British occupation in 1808; a sequel to *Portrait of Clare*; and an epic English history), only *The Island* ever came to fruition. The novels which he did write during the war years (*Mr Lucton's Freedom* and *A Man About the House*) were in response to Heinemann's request for something in a lighter vein. Of the first its author commented:

> It isn't the kind of book I can write or should ever have begun

to write. Partly, I suppose because I don't really believe that
Owen Lucton would ever have left his £2,000 car at the bottom
of the Avon and started a new life; these premises having been
rejected, all the rest becomes bosh.
(FBY 1532)

The second was an admitted pot-boiler, written when Francis was
less than happy about the progress of *The Island*.

As there is no likelihood of the poem being finished or selling
well when it is finished, I had to set about writing something
to pay off my arrears of surtax, a relic of more prosperous
days; so I began a lightish novel about two old ladies in Italy.
(FBY 3077)

As the war came to an end, it was obvious that Brett Young's health
was failing and once again he needed to seek the permanent balm
of a warmer climate. Both of his homes were sold: Talland to a
neighbour, Mrs Browning of Pershore, and Craycombe to a friend,
Lord Cobham of Hagley, and Francis and Jessie prepared to move
to South Africa, 'that beautiful land which I have always loved best
on earth after my own dear Worcestershire' (FBY 1563).

Nine: Africa

Francis Brett Young's fascination with Africa began with the sampler which hung on his nursery wall at The Laurels. His *Kintuck* voyage in 1907 first carried him to the continent's northern shores, and when in 1914 recuperation in a warm climate was prescribed for a severe attack of jaundice, the most readily accessible location was Algiers, where he spent three weeks. Though the wild flowers, the strange architecture and the local population were novel, this was not really Africa and the impression made upon Francis was limited to the 'short respite of calls at Gibralter and Algiers (BR 3)' as Paul Ritchie journeyed to Naples.

When Francis made a close acquaintance with the inhospitable lands of Equatorial Africa during the Tanga campaign, the harshness of climate and conditions sowed a plentiful literary crop. In 1935 Francis returned to North Africa with Jessie, to spend Christmas with Lloyd George in Morocco. Marrakech seemed to offer the ideal climate, and the company, which included Winston Churchill, was stimulating, but Morocco made no more impact upon Brett Young's writing than did Algiers, as the holiday merely provided a diversion during the writing of *Far Forest*.

A first visit to Egypt, during the winter of 1922-23, was made so that Robert Dolbey, then practising in Cairo, might remove Brett Young's troublesome appendix. A period of convalescence permitted Mr and Mrs Brett Young to visit Giza by moonlight, as Mr and Mrs Simeon Jackson would do in 'Glamour', as well as a brief trip to Luxor and the Theban tombs.

Two years later the Brett Youngs made a second visit to Egypt accompanied by Axel Munthe, who had been invited by Howard Carter to inspect the newly-discovered tomb of Tutankhamun. From Cairo, Robert Dolbey led a four-day camel safari through the desert to El Faiyum. Francis's encounter here with a garrulous dragoman

141

was the undoubted inspiration both for Achmet in 'Glamour', and the prejudicial outburst from Hendrik Bezuidenhout to Ruth Morgan: 'I doubt there's any creature lower in the scale of corrupt humanity than the dragoman of the Cairo hotels. A parasite, preying on the old, dead, rotten nonsense of the desert's glamour' (KL 131). When the party moved on to Thebes, the Brett Youngs stayed at the Luxor Hotel, where Ruth would also be refreshed.

> When she had lunched in the cool, quiet, pleasantly shabby dining-room of the Luxor hotel, she walked under a sun-dappled avenue to the Nile embankment.
> (KL 256)

The west bank of the Nile during the 1924-25 season was a hive of activity. Robert Mond had resumed work on Vizier Ramose's tomb (no. 55), first excavated by Villiers Stuart in 1879. During a systematic clearing of the ground towards the Ramesseum, where Ruth would have her final assignation with Bezuidenhout, a sandstone portico supported by four columns flanking the entrance to a previously unknown tomb was discovered. Brett Young, who had not been included with Munthe in Carter's invitation, and had therefore refused to join queuing tourists to pay his respects to Tutankhamun, was invited by Mond to the opening of the tomb (no. 324) of Hatiay from the reign of the nineteenth dynasty Pharaoh, Merenptah.

When Ruth was invited to the opening of the tomb of Henhenet, priestess of Amon, from the eleventh dynasty Pharaoh Mentuhotep, an episode which undoubtedly recalled Brett Young's own experience, the expedition began

> down a precipitous path, where soft earth shelved in sections of loose shale and peaty, stable rubbish, down to the core of limestone. In the pit of the excavation, the very atmosphere was solid with suspended dust. There was just room enough to stand. She saw a half-cleared chamber, hewn in limestone with walls on which carven shapes declared themselves.
> (KL 205-206)

Arriving at the tomb on his visit, Francis was struck by the wall-paintings with their agricultural scenes, and the hieroglyphics which identified Hatiay as High Priest of Sobek and of Mont; overseer of the priests of all the gods.

The mythology of Egypt permeated *The Key of Life*. The readers' awareness of Deir el-Bahri, Queen Hatshepsut, the columns of Amenhotep and the pylons of Karnak was taken for granted. In castigation of Bezuidenhout's revolutionary ideas, Hugh Bredon compared him with Akhenaten, a diminished metaphor for those unacquainted with the story of the apostate pharaoh. When a swarm of bees caused the Colossi of Memnon to 'sing', understanding of the choice of verb to describe this effect was assumed. By Brett Young's own admission, he did not write for nitwits and his sensitivity to atmosphere and subsequent use of it was obvious from his stay in Egypt.

However, before either of the Egyptian visits, Brett Young had made his first exploration of the South Africa which was eventually to become his home. By 1920 the large canvas first envisaged during the Tanga campaign was becoming clearer. 'I want to go to Africa next winter. I have a plan for a big book about the birth of the South African nation centred in Johannesburg' (FBY 786). This proposal, which spawned two additional novels, grew from one big book into a trilogy, for which, during an embryonic twenty years, Francis would read more than one hundred studies of African history.

In February 1921, the Brett Youngs sailed from Naples on the *Carisbrooke Castle*, to stay in Johannesburg with Jessie's sister Nancy and her mining-engineer husband, Alfred Brett. The voyage to Durban took them via the Suez Canal and the Red Sea, down the east coast of Africa, passing Mombassa and Zanzibar, the very route which would be followed by the *Vega*, when Captain Glanvil made his epic journey from Naples to Africa.

A visit, with Alfred Brett, to Pilgrim's Rest, a Transvaal mining town established as a gold diggers' camp some fifty years earlier, suggested a scene which, on a reduced scale, could have disfigured Francis's own Black Country.

> Beneath the towering structure of the headgear all the buildings looked small and squat and human figures seemed puny and contemptible beside the monstrous machinery. Up and down five thousand feet of shaft the skips and cages darted like gigantic shuttles, discharging the workers of the shift that had ended, swallowing in mouthfuls the natives of the down-shift who clustered together like a swarm of bees.
>
> (PR 125)

From the visit to Pilgrim's Rest emerged a novel with the same name, in which the militant trade unionism and industrial violence which shook the Rand in 1913, and raged again during Brett Young's visit, were recreated in the fictional Diadem and Brak Deep mines. The skills and conditions of work of Jack Hayman, the ganger-hero of the story were described with an accuracy and awareness which came, no doubt, from Alfred Brett and his associates.

> The coils burned at the rate of a foot a minute, and by careful graduation the moment of each explosion could be timed almost to the second. The law provided that at the moment of firing each entrance to the stope must have its guard. Hayman picked up his tchisa-stick, a piece of wood round the end of which a strip of gelignite had been bound, and lit it at the white flame of his lamp. Next he passed from hole to hole and lit the hanging fuses in order of their length.
> (PR 207)

The leisure pursuits of Johannesburg were also recounted. Though Jessie, with Nancy and Alfred Brett, obviously entered into the spirit of the occasion, Jack Hayman expressed Francis's jingoistic distaste for the enthusiastic reception given to a native jazz band at a Saturday night dance.

> One by one the dancers, exhausted, reeled back to their chairs. Only in the kraals of Mashonaland had Hayman seen such abandonment to the intoxication of rhythm. Never had he imagined that people of European race could be so possessed. It shamed him.
> (PR 325-326)

During this year-long visit, the Brett Youngs spent a protracted vacation near Somerset West, at the Vergelegen estate of Sir Lionel Phillips, the mining magnate, and his wife Florence, art connoisseur and social reformer, to whom *City of Gold* would later be dedicated. Here, while Jessie acted as Lady Phillips' secretary, Francis fished and wrote. *Woodsmoke*, which earned its author an advance of four hundred and twenty-six pounds, was dedicated to Nancy and Alfred Brett, in whose house it was begun, and told the story of the early history of the N'dalo goldfield, leading up to the events of *Pilgrim's Rest*.

Whilst in Johannesburg, Brett Young's time was greatly occupied in the Rand Club Library, absorbing South African history; having moved to Vergelegen, his studies were transferred to the Cape Town Library. In the company of Sir Lionel and Lady Phillips, Francis and Jessie explored Cape Province, visiting Cape Town's Art Gallery, which Francis found particularly noteworthy.

> In the modern streets and squares you may stumble on examples of Colonial architecture, with finely proportioned facades, pilasters and pediments, carefully preserved to remind citizens of today of their forebear's more gracious manner of life. Such is the Michaelis Gallery, which contains a fine collection of pictures of its own sedate period.
>
> (ISA 30)

Welgelegen, home of the dynastic Prinsloos was an obvious echo of Vergelegen, visited during the Brett Youngs' stay by Cathleen Mann, future exhibitor at the Royal Academy and official Second World War artist. The somewhat whimsical portrait of Francis which she painted at Lady Phillips's expense, was presented to the University of Birmingham after his death.

Ten years would pass before Brett Young continued his literary pilgrimage to Southern Africa. In March 1931, having sailed to Beira in Southern Rhodesia, Francis and Jessie made the Salisbury home of Colonel Essex Capell their base for a three-month exploration of the Zambesi. Though seeking information for his projected South Africa trilogy, Francis was currently writing *Mr & Mrs Pennington*, set in Hales Owen's contemporary, semi-detached suburbs. Discovering in Ada Road, Salisbury, new bungalows unjustifiably dignified with the names of English stately homes, he transferred the whole architectural masquerade to Tilton (Quinton, near Hales Owen), locating his hero and heroine in 'Chatsworth' and their neighbours in 'Welbeck' and 'Belvoir'.

Provided, through the good offices of Capell, with a government car and driver, the Brett Youngs set off to explore Rhodesia. Umtali made a favourable impression which produced a florid description.

> Its well-watered gardens nourish all kinds of tropical and sub-tropical fruits and its wide streets bordered by vermilion-flowered spathodeas and flamboyant acacias are among the most opulent sights of Southern Rhodesia.
>
> (ISA 120)

The ancient history of the country was encountered at the acropolis of Great Zimbabwe, concerning the enigmatic and legendary origins of which, Brett Young remained cautiously agnostic.

> Nobody knows for certain when, or by whom it was built. The only certainty is that these ruins, in bulk and lonely grandeur, constitute the most impressive monument of antiquity in all Southern Africa.
> (ISA 111)

This trip also gave Francis his first sight of the 'smoke that thunders' — the Victoria Falls — which, he was happy to concede, were among the most impressive spectacles not just in Southern Africa, but in the world. 'The stupefying impression of titanic power and magnitude which they make cannot be forgotten. It remains in one's mind and haunts it' (ISA 121).

The third visit to South Africa was designed with research in mind: to explore the route of the Great Trek a century earlier, which would be the basis of the first movement of what he intended to be a symphony of Africa; but also to prepare the script which Brett Young hoped to write for Basil Dean's intended film of the birth of the South African nation. Having purchased a Ford Utility van specially for the expedition, Francis and Jessie, accompanied by their Craycombe chauffeur, Harry Little, and Giles Bromley-Martin, set sail aboard the *Edinburgh Castle* in February 1936. Arriving in Cape Town, Francis renewed his acquaintance with General Smuts, who provided him with letters of introduction to Lt Col. James Stevenson-Hamilton, the curator of the Kruger National Park.

Having travelled from Cape Town to Queenstown and crossed the path of the Voortrekkers, who had taken the northern route around the Drakensberg Mountains, Brett Young's party skirted to the south. Here they encountered their first difficulty. Rain had turned the road from Maclear to Matatiele into mud, the Ford Utility van making no easier progress than did John Grafton's wagon.

> Every brook that crossed their path was a foaming torrent; the wide track became nothing but a series of pools and morasses in which the spans slithered, finding no foothold, and wagon-wheels sank.
> (TSC 615)

From Pietermaritzburg, Brett Young followed the Tugela Valley, where Dingaan's Zulus decimated Pieter Retief's Voortrekkers and where the Prinsloo trek would be destroyed, over Van Reenan's Pass and on toward Potchefstroom and the Witwatersrand where the Grafton family were still settled in *City of Gold*.

At Skukuza in the Kruger Park, the Brett Young party stayed with Stevenson-Hamilton and spent some time on safari, before crossing into Rhodesia. The intention was to continue north, retracing the route of the Tanga campaign, before returning home from Mombassa. Heavy rains however had closed the road into Tanganyika and this plan had to be abandoned. At Lusaka, they were guests of the Governor of Northern Rhodesia, Sir Hubert Young, at the opening of parliament. The continuing rainy season meant that progress to Fort Jameson was slow, with tribesmen frequently coming to the rescue to dig the van out of the engulfing mud. Though an encounter with two lions passed without harm, the incident, through which Brett Young slept, alerted him to the ease with which a lion would kill a horse belonging to the sleeping John Grafton. When the party eventually reached Nyasaland, roads to the north were still blocked and all bridges down. A journey through Dedza, Zomba, Blantyre, Tete and Moko brought them back to Salisbury and on to Beira and England. Even though Francis had been totally immersed in the atmosphere of Southern Africa during the past four months and seven thousand miles, the homeward voyage on the *SS Madura* was spent completing *Far Forest*, a novel which never strayed beyond the borderlands of his birth.

Two years later, in a cottage belonging to his old friend Florence Phillips in Montagu in the Lesser Karroo, Francis found opportunity for continued preparation for the projected trilogy, which he had begun to consider his attempt at *War and Peace*. Here was also respite from the demands of his current novel. *Dr Bradley Remembers* recalled a career in general practice, which in both length and period matched that of Dr Thomas Brett Young, who died in March 1938 whilst Francis was still in South Africa.

Brett Young's reading list for 1937 indicated how assiduous was his research. Background material included the monumental studies of George McCall Theal; *The History of South Africa* by Eric Walker; *The Rise of South Africa* by George Cory; *Travels in Southern Africa* by H. Lichtenstein. Specific regions were covered by Aylwood's *The Transvaal of Today*; Fitzpatrick's *The Transvaal from Within*; *Annals of Natal* by J. Bird. *L'Expansion des Boers au XIXe Siècle* by H. Deherain;

The Native Policy of the Voortrekkers by J. Agar-Hamilton; *Trek Across the Drakensberg* by Louis Trigardt; *The Great Trek* by E.A. Walker dealt with the influence and movement of Dutch South Africans, whilst Ian Colvin's *Life of Dr Jameson* and Sarah Millin's *Cecil John Rhodes* provided vital information about key historical figures.

They Seek a Country and *City of Gold* (originally entitled *Ridge of White Waters*) along with an unwritten third volume in which

> I shall have to deal with the Second Boer War, and with such embarrassing subjects as Concentration Camps, a formidable prospect from which bolder men than myself might well shrink,
>   (TSC Preface xiii)

exemplified the weaving together of fact and fiction at which Brett Young was adept. Pieter Retief, Gerhardus Maritz, Hendrik Potgeiter, Andries Pretorious and Pieter Uys of the Great Trek were significant in the earlier novel, in which Blood River was a turning-point for the fictional Voortrekkers as for their originals. The bungled executions at Slachter's Nek were recalled in *They Seek a Country* by Jan Bothma, whose cousin, Stephanus, was cast as one of the revolutionaries to be hanged twice, while Frederick Bezuidenhout, the actual instigator of the 1815 insurrection, gave his name to one of the families who trekked with the Prinsloos. Chaka, Dingaan and Cetewayo, Zulu kings; Sekukuni, Chief of the Bapedi and Barney Barnato, mining magnate, all featured in Brett Young's saga. President Kruger, Cecil Rhodes and Dr Jameson were pivotal characters in *City of Gold*. The fictional John Grafton fought at Blood River in the first novel, whilst his son, Piet, was credited with the idea of the ill-fated Jameson raid in the second. The years of preparation devoted to Brett Young's African symphony were acknowledged in his *Cape Times* obituary, which allowed that though neither of his novels of South Africa gave any great original insight into the Union's history, they showed industrious research and a determination not to be slipshod or superficial in approach.

When it became apparent after a serious heart attack in October 1944 that Brett Young needed the permanent balm of a warm climate, South Africa was the chosen haven. War-time passages were not easily obtained, and even with the influence of General Smuts, it was July 1945 before Francis renewed his acquaintance with the Blue Funnel Line, when the *Nesta* carried him to Cape Town, where he and Jessie moved into the Majestic Hotel, Kalk Bay. The reasons for his decision were obvious.

> Southern Africa contains some of the loveliest and most spectacular scenery in the world; its climate is undoubtedly healthy. For the elderly or the invalid the choice cannot be bettered.
> (ISA 132)

As far as the decision affected South Africa, the *Cape Times* recognised that in Brett Young's coming, the country gladly received as faithful an immigrant as it had ever welcomed.

The inactivity of failing health brought compensations: cricket at Newlands; Thursday morning rehearsals of the Cape Town Municipal Orchestra conducted by Enrique Jorda; reading in Cape Town Library. However recent years had taken other tolls. His books were largely out of print; royalties yielded only a fraction of pre-war income; double taxation crippled English writers resident in South Africa. Three projects motivated Francis: the final volume of the South African trilogy, another Mercian novel and his autobiography, for which he planned to write pen portraits of some of his numerous correspondents. Aspirations for his South African writing were that it would play a part in shaping the nation. 'I am anxious to finish this big work which I have always hoped may be of some use in promoting racial understanding in South Africa' (FBY 3238). A part in shaping the nation was assured when the Natal Education Department set for its Junior Examinations *They Seek a Country*, which with *City of Gold* was published in a South Africa Educational Edition. In private Brett Young's prejudices and anxieties for the future of his adopted homeland were expressed to his old friend Humphrey Humphreys.

> The rising tide of colour is lapping our feet and the return of the Nationalist Government has made the coloureds truculent, though God knows the Cape coloured people are generally highly-paid.
> (FBY 2868)

Of the three proposed works only the Midlands novel, which would fill a final gap, became a reality.

> I have dealt with every grade of society except the nobility.

The new book is about a Worcestershire family of landowners
in the decline of the last twenty years. I think it will take a
worthy place in the Mercian series.
(FBY 1581)

This autobiographical novel, *Wistanslow*, though never finished, was
published posthumously in its incomplete form in 1956, Francis's
link with the plot being clearly established. 'The book is about John
Folliott. When I appear in it, it is when I am so near that I cast a
shadow' (FBY 17).

After almost two years at the Majestic Hotel, the Brett Youngs
moved into Leighton Road, St James, where their new cottage,
Alacen (a contraction of previous owners' names, for which Francis
quickly substituted Leighton House) overlooked the sea. A new
writing/music room was built and from England came their furniture
and Francis's books, sadly damaged owing to mishandling in transit.
Invited by the South African Tourist Corporation to write a study of
the country for prospective visitors and settlers, Francis embarked
upon what was to be his final African safari, gathering information
and refreshing his memory for what was to be his final complete
book, *In South Africa*.

The hilly terrain of St James proved an unfortunate choice for
someone with a heart condition, and it became necessary to move
again, this time to a thatched cottage in De Kock Street, Montagu
South, in a peaceful wine and fruit-growing valley of Alpine qualities
in the Lesser Karroo.

> Our cottage is surrounded by acres of veld, most
> astonishingly flowered in spring and winter. The house is girt
> by a small, fertile garden zone, which grows oranges, grape-
> fruit, lemons, guavas, vines and even paw-paws.
> (FBY 2869)

Here, during a drought, Francis dowsed for water, as his ancestors
had frequently done and as Edwin Ingleby once did, 'with his hands
turned palm upwards, the arms of the twig between the third and
fourth fingers, the thumb, and the palm of each hand, and the fork
downwards between them' (YP 216). At the place where the twig
broke in Francis's hands, water was found at a depth of 169 feet,
justification of words written more than thirty years before. 'Edwin
was curiously thrilled with the whole business. It was better, he

thought, to be born a dowser than a Fellow of Balliol' (YP 216). The original architect of the Montagu house was commissioned to add a library, but Brett Young could not sustain the strain of creativity, and he would write no more.

Disgruntled by declining popularity and the suspicion of official neglect, 'not even my own sooty Alma Mater has ever set the seal of its approval of my work on me', (FBY 2597) he nevertheless consented to travel to England when in 1950, as part of its Golden Jubilee celebrations, this omission was rectified and the University of Birmingham conferred the honorary degree of Doctor of Letters upon Francis Brett Young, who was lauded by the Public Orator (Professor Thomas Bodkin) as the most accomplished artist whom the University had yet produced.

As his health continued to decline, Francis was unable to undertake public engagements or deal with his own correspondence. In January 1954 he was admitted to the Tamboerskloof Nursing Home in Cape Town, where the few visitors he received were carefully monitored by Jessie. In the early hours of 28 March 1954, Francis Brett Young died of hypertensive cardiac failure, his estate, valued at seventeen thousand pounds (a modest financial reward for forty years of literary outpouring), passing absolutely to his widow. His funeral, conducted by the Dean of Cape Town, Very Rev. M. Gibbs, was held two days later in St George's Cathedral, followed by cremation at Maitland Crematorium. In accordance with his wishes, on 3 July 1954, his ashes were interred in the north transept of Worcester Cathedral, where a burial place between the relics of St Wulstan and St Oswald expedited resurrection for King John who, in the very words chosen to introduce the memorial service for his creator, declared

> I commend
> My body and soul to God and to Saint Wulstan.
> (I 128)

So, through the mouth of the thirteenth century monk John de Mathon, Francis proclaimed his own eternal hope.

> When the trumpet sounds
> And the graves give up their dead,
> He might take his place
> In the bright company of Heaven.
> (I 128)

Religion was part of Brett Young's story. Attendance at Hales Owen Church was a childhood reality which he shared with Edwin Ingleby and Richard Verdon. It was, however, an aesthetic and cultural experience rather than a spiritual one. The appeal of 'our little cathedral' lay in the grandeur of its architecture, the resonance of the rector's voice, the soaring notes of the organ; the congregational psalmody. Here all the joys and sorrows of the towns were gathered together to be offered, not to God, but to any interested observer who happened to be present. 'In a small community such as ours the church became a stage on which, in a superb Gothic setting, the tragi-comedy of village life was enacted' (W 8-9).

It was at Hales Owen and Epsom College that Brett Young absorbed the ancient canticles and liturgies of the church which frequently illuminated his writing. Psalm 121 came to his aid as he agonized over the futility of war:

> Unto the hills, O God, unto the hills
> From whence a dream of childhood comes of late...
> Unto the hills, unto the hills I bring
> My soul for soothing of their solitude.
>   (FBY 67)

In the first ecstasies of Clare's marriage to Ralph Hingston, the implied but unwritten passion was conveyed by a biblical reference: '"My beloved is mine and I am his." Through the death of winter, Clare sang her Song of Songs' (PC 262). A similar technique was used when she announced her intention of marrying Dudley Wilburn, bringing to fruition her aunt's long-cherished ambitions. 'Aunt Cathie's heart sang its "Nunc Dimittis"' (PC 415).

Against a family background of agnosticism, the teenage Clare underwent an intensely emotional religious experience of Anglo-Catholicism, characteristic of the late nineteenth century. At a similar stage in her life Francis's sister Doris began the exploration of Anglo-Catholic worship, which would result in her being received into the Church of Rome.

Suspicious of all organised religion, Brett Young was particularly hostile to the Anglo-Catholic tradition. The anti-papal suspicions of Miss Loach regarding the dress and churchmanship of Chaddesbourne's new vicar may be dismissed as the out-dated prejudices of a finely-drawn character.

> She frowned on the biretta, because it suggested doctrinal

flirtations with the Scarlet Woman, the Whore of Babylon. Though she knew they existed, she was glad that she had never set eyes on candles and vestments.

(TLW 30)

The irreligious Aunt Cathy's view of Father Darnay was only to be expected.

'I don't know this Mr Darnay personally, but I've heard enough to form an opinion. A Romanizer, a Papist, who hasn't the courage to "go over". A great favourite with women. No doubt he enjoys their confessions. Spiritual flirtations: that's what I call them.'

(PC 74)

However, when Clare received communion from him, it was not a character, but the author himself who spoke these derisive words.

Her hands trembled as she held them out to receive the wafer which Darnay, mumbling his formula, placed in her palm.

(PC 725)

In marked contrast to his sister, in his late teenage years Francis steadfastly refused to be confirmed, even though his father arranged for him to be interviewed at the newly-consecrated Birmingham Cathedral, the architecture of which so impressed the young John Bradley when first he saw

an ancient graveyard thickset with carved urns and obelisks and other memorials of the Georgian dead, from the midst of which there rose the ornate sandstone cupola of the church in which they had worshipped, a shape of classical beauty dreamily poised above the dark city.

(DBR 122)

Clare and Steven were both confirmed, this being for Clare the predictable expression of a passing stage.

When she was at St Monica's, Clare got into the hands of some High Church woman who worried her into being confirmed. It's quite common with schoolgirls, that emotional religious phase.

(PC 162)

For Steven, it was the logical outcome of an absorbing interest, which evolved from curiosity into bigotry.

> Steven, fired by the influence of the priest who had prepared him for confirmation, was as earnestly concerned with the findings of the Council of Trent as with the rules of the Rugby Union.
> (PC 501)

With her marriage, Clare came to realise that religion had dominated her life, because her emotions had previously found no other means of expression. 'Never had she seen Ralph pray in private; and though the omission had once mildly shocked her, she now knew he was none the worse for it' (PC 282). However for another young husband, Dick Pennington, daily prayer was a ritual to be maintained even in a prison cell.

> Something important had been neglected: he realised that for the first time in his life, he had forgotten to pray. He knelt down and said the Lord's Prayer; and, being a simple soul, was greatly comforted.
> (MMP 557)

Though Marmaduke Considine once preached an unusually well-constructed sermon, and Canon Lingen of Temple Folliott and Rev. Malthus of Cold Orton were exceptions, Brett Young's clerics were generally vainglorious. Mr Pomfret, the Vicar of Wychbury, the furnishings of whose study 'proclaimed his prowess as oarsman rather than as scholar or divine' (PC 60) was nonplussed when Clare applied to him for confirmation. When conducting his second cousin's funeral, he 'boomed the burial service and looked, in his surplice, like a hunting man in fancy dress' (WL 520). Clerical reticence raised a permanent barrier between Mr Follows and his flock.

> When he ascends the pulpit, the sermon he preaches is the paraphrase of a biblical text for schoolchildren or some definition of doctrine for their elders — not a confession of the doubts that are burning his heart.
> (PV 177)

Mr Jewell of Thorpe Folville, 'a tall, slovenly man, with a big beard, smelling of tobacco, who snorted as he breathed through a moustache that appeared to grow up into his nostrils', (JR 47) and his colleague, Mr Holly of Rossington, 'a plump, white-handed bachelor whose intimate feminine humour flattered the ladies' (JR 47) were not caricatures, but characters drawn from life. 'Most of my scenes from clerical life were absorbed from the parsons of those Leicestershire villages who made up the greater part of our rural society in the nineties' (FBY 2594).

The greatest clerical opprobrium was reserved for Father Darnay. 'I disliked Mr Darnay's aura of incense and Anglicanism, which some Protestant strain in my nature instinctively distrusted' (W 16). Goaded by the priest, whom he rightly distrusted, Richard Verdon relived an actual boyhood episode when Francis defended Hales Owen's poet, as he declaimed, 'a passage of turgid blank verse from Shenstone's "Lines on a Distant Prospect of Halesby Abbey", in which the poet (with feelings as anti-clerical as were mine at that moment) rejoiced in its Dissolution' (W 17-18). It was not only the title of 'The Ruined Abbey' with which Brett Young took liberties. Verdon's quotation reached its climax with the lines

> ... the luxurious priest
> Crawl'd from his bedded strumpet, muttering low
> An ineffectual curse.
> (W 18)

What Shenstone actually wrote was 'each angry friar'; Brett Young's substitution of 'the luxurious priest' being not an unintentional misquote, but a deliberately harsh indictment of Father Darnay and all he represented.

The religiously-inclined laity fared little better, whether the canting humbug of Thirza Moule who having abandoned her father to his fate in a torrential storm, that she might rescue his money, 'sank to her knees and prayed aloud to the God who had bidden His chosen to spoil the Egyptians' (FF 362) or the pretensions of Mr Silley who, in the Chapel of Brixham's United Methodists,

> prayed that those who had been out in that terrible gale, should have vouchsafed to them the miracle of the Sea of Galilee. Mr Silley had an aptitude for this particular language; he was inspired by the sound of his own voice.
> (DS 288)

As befitted the dignity and social status of a respected Medical Officer of Health, Dr Thomas Brett Young served a term as Church Warden at Hales Owen, where Francis occasionally acted as sidesman, a role also fulfilled by Mr Ingleby and those leading members of the Halesby community, Sir Joseph Hingston and Walter Willis. Dr Verdon however, 'like most medical men, was a stalwart agnostic, who went to church merely as a civic duty and as an example to souls more timid' (W 37).

From the security of her own religious certainties, Francis's sister Doris confessed, after his death, that she had never thought of her brother as a believing Christian, an assessment he confirmed in a personal statement.

> Though I have a profound distrust of all formal religion, I do not think it would be fair to say that I am not a religious man. My life has been devoid of what is called religious experience.
>   (FBY 2594)

To the amiable Dr Selby was accorded the privilege of making the clearest statement of Brett Young's own position.

> I come to church, first of all, because the building is beautiful, and because I find the Anglican liturgy sublime. I come because I believe in tradition and continuity of experience. Then I come because it's a good example; I think the beauty and quietude and all the other things I find there, are good for the soul. Lastly, I come because I enjoy it. As for the mystical part of religion, I'm not really religious. Those things mean nothing to me; they're left out of my composition.
>   (TLW 114-5)

Though for Francis Brett Young organised religion was either a palliative cordial for impressionable girls, bigots and simple souls, or a matter of social propriety by which the Established Church maintained the established structures; though, by his own admission, lacking any meaningful spiritual experience, when expressing his most deeply-held convictions, Francis chose the vehicle of religious terminology.

The first profession of his creed was truth. 'If I were asked to rewrite the Shorter Catechism, I should say that the whole duty of man is to seek for Truth' (FBY 57). The second profession was creative achievement. In a paper to which he gave an explicitly religious title, 'Sweet Content — A Lay Sermon', Francis described what he considered to be this highest of all human attributes.

> Happiness consists in giving expression to the desire to create which, simply because we are human, is latent in all of us. That is our principal justification for being alive. This is the Divine Dispensation: that we are rewarded according to our own capacity for creative achievement.
> (FBY 64)

The third profession was the belief that the creative expression of truth was a worthy undertaking. 'Every book that a serious artist writes is, in some degree, an Act of Faith' (TSC Preface vi).

> Though I was once a doctor (ubi tres medici, ibi duo athei), I can say that every book I have written is, in a sense, an Act of Faith.
> (FBY 3465)

The truth of the stories to which, through more than forty years and more than forty books, Francis Brett Young's creative achievement gave birth, was undergirded by his own life story and by the wider story of which he was part. The Act of Faith was that both for himself and for his readers, his was a story worth telling.

> My lingering task is done;
> My tale is told...
> And this I claim:
> In all my story there has been no page
> Brighter than this: we have lived in a great age.
> (I 451)

Chronology

1884   29 June: Birth of Francis Brett Young
24 August: Baptised at St John's Church, Hales Owen

1891   Entered Iona Cottage High School, Sutton Coldfield

1895   Played violin solo at Iona School Concert
Entered Epsom College

1898   27 June: Death of mother (Annie Elizabeth Young)

1899   Elected to Epsom College Debating Society
Read Kipling's 'The Absent-Minded Beggar' at Epsom College Literary
    Evening

1900   Editor of 'The Epsomian'
Passed Higher Certificate Examination

1901   26 February: Marriage of father (Thomas Brett Young) and Margaret
    Allan
February: Conducted Carr House Choir
July: Roseberry Prize for English Literature
Entered University of Birmingham with Sands Cox Scholarship

1904   Met Jessie Hankinson at Assembly Rooms, Edgbaston

1905   Lodged with Gertrude Dale at 105, Harborne Road, Birmingham
25 June: Proposed to Jessie at Leasowes
Jessie took up teaching post at Sidcot
December: Secretly engaged to Jessie

1906   March: Lodged in Bath Row, Birmingham during midwifery course
August: Assisted Dr George Bryce in Aston
November: Qualified as doctor
Officially engaged to Jessie
Signed on with Alfred Holt & Co., Liverpool

1907   5 January: Sailed for Japan and China as ship's doctor on SS *Kintuck*
9 May: Disembarked at London
Holiday at Hawkshead with Jessie, chaperoned by Gertrude Dale
June/July: Locum to Dr William McCall at Hockley
August: Locum to Dr James McDonald at Bloxwich

September: Borderlands walking holiday with Alfred Hayes
October: Partnership with Dr Quicke, Brixham (Lodged at Cumbers)

1908   Moved into Cleveland House, New Road, Brixham
March: Opened additional surgery at Galmpton
28 December: Married Jessie Hankinson at St Michael's Church, Rowberrow
(Honeymoon at Skelwith Bridge, Westmorland)

1911   Summer walking tour in Welsh Marches with Jessie

1912   Performed emergency tracheotomy at Brixham Cottage Hospital
Songs of Robert Bridges (Breitkopf & Hartel)

1913   February: *Songs for Voice and Pianoforte* (Weekes & Co.)
Martin Secker became British publisher
September: *Undergrowth* (with Eric Brett Young)

1914   February: *Deep Sea*
Recuperated in Algiers after attack of jaundice
Moved to Old Garden House, Berry Head
September: *Robert Bridges: A Critical Study* (with Eric Brett Young)

1915   February: *The Dark Tower*

1916   1 January: Commissioned Lieutenant in RAMC
2 January: Posted to No 2 Camp, Sling, near Bulford, Salisbury Plain
March: *The Iron Age*
1 April: Sailed for Cape Town
21 April: Sailed on to Mombassa
8 May: Transferred to Indian Hospital, Nairobi
14 May: Attached to 2nd Rhodesian Regiment
21 May: Began march toward Tanga
9-10 June: Lost in bush at M'Kalamo
24 June: Ordered back to Handeni Hospital with malaria
5 July: Returned to action
1 August: Ordered back to Handeni with recurrent malaria
(Transferred to Voi Base Hospital and then to Nairobi)
14 August: Convalescent at Lady Colville's Nursing Home, Nairobi
26 August: Discharged for duties at Indian General Hospital, Nairobi
8 September: Seconded to Maharajah Scindia of Gwalior's Convalescent Home

1917   20 January: Dislocated forearm in riding accident
28 January: Sailed for Egypt
17 February: Arrived Bristol
Treatment at Military Hospital, Devonport
Appointed Registrar at Military Hospital, Tidworth
Convalescence in Ireland
June: *Five Degrees South*

September: *Marching on Tanga* (Collins)

1918   March: *The Crescent Moon*

1919   January: Dutton & Co published first American edition (*The Crescent Moon*)

Moved to Capri, leased Villa Rosaio at Anacapri from Edwin Cerio (also casetta at Piccola Marina from Compton Mackenzie)

W. Collins replaced Martin Secker as British publisher

First appearance in *Georgian Poetry*, edited by Edward Marsh

May: *Crepe de Chine* performed privately at Kingsway Theatre, London, transferred to Repertory Theatre, Plymouth, where *The Third Sex* also produced; *One of the Family* first produced at Gaiety Theatre, Manchester

June: *Captain Swing* (with W.E. Stirling), produced at Plymouth, May 26

October: *The Young Physician*

December: *Poems 1916-1918*

1920   Bought Villa Fraita, Anacapri, from Antonino Mazarella

Visited Sicily with D.H. Lawrence

Edward Marsh began proof-reading FBY's works

September: *The Tragic Bride* (Martin Secker)

1921   February: First South African visit; stayed with Nancy and Alfred Brett in Johannesburg, Florence and Lionel Phillips at Vergelegen

The Black Diamond

October: *The Red Knight*

18 December: First amateur production of *The Furnace* at The Haymarket

Crepe de Chine: The Story of the Play with W.E. Stirling (Mills & Boon)

1922   January: Portrait painted by Cathleen Mann at Vergelegen

February: Returned to Capri

November: *Pilgrim's Rest*

December: Visited Cairo for appendectomy

1923   January: Visited Luxor and excavations at Thebes

1924   April: *Woodsmoke*

November: *Cold Harbour*

1925   January: Second Egyptian visit; opening of Tomb of Hatiay

Cassell and Co. replaced W. Collins as British publisher

Alfred A. Knopf replaced E.P. Dutton & Co. as American publisher

May: *Sea Horses*

1926   September: Heinemann replaced Cassell as British publisher

December: Sailed for New York for American Lecture Tour

1927   March: *Portrait of Clare*

Won James Tait Black Memorial Prize

April: Returned to Capri

1928   February: *The Key of Life*
October: *My Brother Jonathan*
November: *The Furnace* (with W. Armstrong) first produced: Liverpool
December: Second American Lecture Tour

1929   February: Returned to Capri via England
July: Leased Esthwaite Lodge, Hawkshead
Harper & Brothers replaced Alfred A. Knopf as American publisher
September: *Black Roses*

1930   6 May: Addressed English Association at University of Birmingham
October: *Jim Redlake*

1931   January: Gave evidence at trial of Alfredo Mazarella, Naples
March-May: Second South African visit (Rhodesia); stayed with Essex Capell
October: *Mr & Mrs Pennington*

1932   January: Louis Golding dedicated *Magnolia Street* to FBY
June: Bought Craycombe House, Fladbury
September: *The House Under The Water*
November: *Blood Oranges* (White Owl Press)

1933   June: Addressed A.G.M. of Friends of Pershore Abbey
July: *The Cage Bird*
10 August: Created Bard 'Claerwenydd' at Wrexham Gorsedd
October: Compton Mackenzie dedicated *Literature In My Time* to FBY
October-November: Cruise aboard *HMS Hood*

1934   July: First Severn Editions
July: *This Little World*
October: Addressed Faculty of Medicine, University of Birmingham
Elected President of Cheltenham Literary Society
John Moore dedicated *Country Men* to FBY
Elected Vice President of Worcestershire Association

1935   25 February: Elected Vice Chairman of Worcestershire Branch of Council for Preservation of Rural England
22 June: Appointed to Executive Committee of Friends of Worcester Cathedral
July: *White Ladies*
Addressed AGM of Friends of Tewkesbury Abbey
Wishart published Twitchett's critical study: *Francis Brett Young*
18 September: Craycombe House opened in aid of Queen's Hospital
27 November: Read 'The Doctor in Literature' to Royal Society of Literature

Christmas in Morocco with Lloyd George

1936 February: Third South African visit: followed route of Great Trek
May: Returned to England
Reynal & Hitchcock replaced Harper & Brothers as American publisher
Bought Talland House
August: *Far Forest*
Joined Worcestershire Archaeological Society

1937 31 July: Garden Party at Craycombe House for Worcestershire Association
August: *They Seek A Country*
December: *Portrait of a Village*
Elected to Council of Friends of Tewkesbury Abbey
Elected to Council of Worcestershire Historical Society

1938 January-April: Fourth South African visit: stayed at Montagu
2 March: Death of father
July: Opened new wing of Birmingham Throat Hospital
August: *Dr Bradley Remembers*
November: *The Christmas Box*
Elected Vice President of Worcestershire County Cricket Club

1939 August: *The City of Gold*
Elected President of Midland Federation of Ramblers' Association

1940 February: *Cotswold Honey*
Craycombe House handed over to Red Cross
September: *Mr Lucton's Freedom*

1942 July: *A Man About The House*
Appointed Chairman of Looe Civil Defence Committee

1944 October: First heart attack
November: *The Island*

1945 July: Emigrated to South Africa; stayed at Majestic Hotel, Kalk Bay

1947 May: Moved to Leighton Road, St James
September-October: Tour of South Africa

1948 Moved to De Kock Street, Montagu South

1949 Sold Villa Fraita, Anacapri

1950 5 May: D. Litt at Golden Jubilee celebrations of University of Birmingham
October: Found water by dowsing on land at Montagu

1951 March-August: Visit to England, France, Tunis, Italy, Switzerland

1952 July: *In South Africa*
July-September: Visit to England

1953 June-July: Final visit to England

CHRONOLOGY

1954   16 January: Admitted to Tamboerskloof Nursing Home, Cape Town
28 March: Death of Francis Brett Young
30 March: Funeral at St George's Cathedral, cremation at Maitland
3 July: Ashes interred in Worcester Cathedral

1956   July: *Wistanslow*

1962   Heinemann published Jessie's biography: *Francis Brett Young*

1966   16 October: Plaque unveiled in Hales Owen Church

1969   University of Rouen published Jacques Leclaire's critical study: *Un Temoin de l'Avenement de l'Angleterre Contemporaine: Francis Brett Young*

1970   2 September: Death of Jessie Brett Young

1973   April: Plaque placed in Hales Owen Magistrates Court (site of birthplace)

1979   2 March: Francis Brett Young Society formed; President: Joan Hassall

1984   21 July: FBY Society placed plaque at Esthwaite Lodge
19 November: Brett Young (Social Services) Day Centre, Hales Owen opened

1985   11 May: FBY Society placed plaque at Epsom College

1992   6 May: FBY Society placed plaque at 105, Harborne Road, Birmingham

1994   29 April: FBY Society placed plaque at Old Garden House, Berry Head

1995   6 May: FBY Society placed plaque at Cleveland House, Brixham

Bibliography

Manuscripts in University of Birmingham Library

Notebooks, diaries and speeches of Francis Brett Young
FBY17 Notebook for *Wistanslow*
FBY23 Notes for proposed autobiography
FBY25 'A Capri Galaxy'
FBY32 'Echo Augury — Call of Africa' 1920
FBY41 'My Garden'
FBY49 'Zambesi'
FBY55 Friends of Tewkesbury Abbey AGM 27.07.1935
FBY56 American lecture tour 1927
FBY57 Birmingham Throat Hospital, 08.1938
FBY62 Ministry of Information, 19.09.1940
FBY64 'Sweet Content: A Lay Sermon'
FBY67 Poems written in East Africa 1916
FBY88 Notebook for *The Black Diamond*
FBY93 Miscellaneous musical compositions
FBY96 Diary 1928
FBY112 'With Chinese Coolies'

Letters of Francis Brett Young
To Jessie Hankinson (Brett Young):
FBY162 14.09.1905; FBY163 15.09.1905; FBY166 22.09.1905; FBY173 22.10.1905; FBY175 10.1905; FBY179 21.11.1905; FBY180 26.11.1905; FBY185 24.12.1905; FBY186 31.12.1905; FBY191 17.01.1906; FBY224 03.1906; FBY249 28.06.1906; FBY252 30.06.1906; FBY256 04.07.1906; FBY274 17.09.1906; FBY312 04.01.1907; FBY317 09.02.1907; FBY325 18.03.1907; FBY327 19-23.04.1907; FBY328 31.03.1907; FBY332 18.06.1907; FBY336 04.07.1907; FBY349 02.11.1907; FBY367 03.03.1908; FBY369 21.03.1908; FBY403 30.07.1908; FBY422 16.12.1908; FBY431 Undated; FBY432 Undated; FBY443 Undated; FBY456 03.01.1916; FBY461 Undated; FBY479 04.05.1916; FBY480 06.05.1916; FBY528 06.11.1916; FBY530 11.11.1916

BIBLIOGRAPHY

To J.B. Pinker:
FBY765 21.06.1919; FBY781 10.12.1919; FBY786 02.1920; FBY821 07.1921;
FBY824 06.08.1921; FBY889 24.11.1923; FBY894 25.01.1924; FBY956
02.07.1926; FBY964 02.09.1926; FBY973 01.1927

To Charles Evans:
FBY1519 13.02.1933; FBY1520 06.04.1934; FBY1521 23.07.1934; FBY1526
05.04.1937; FBY1530 11.09.1939; FBY1532 01.01.1940; FBY1538 23.07.1940;
FBY1549 13.07.1941; FBY1531 05.12.1939; FBY1541 25.11.1940

To Martin Secker:
FBY1678 19.11.1914; FBY1688 02.06.1916; FBY1697 24.10.1916; FBY1724
31.10.1919; FBY1727 10.01.1920; FBY1730 06.02.1920

To various correspondents:
FBY567 Dr T.B. Young 10.1919
FBY1108 Doubleday & Co. 22.11.1948
FBY1563 Charles Morgan 02.09.1947
FBY1581 A.S. Frere 25.01.1947
FBY1594 A.S. Frere 24.01.1950
FBY1853 H.B.M. Consul, Naples 20.10.1944
FBY2145 Charles Morgan 19.07.1934
FBY2228 J.C. Smuts 25.12.1920
FBY2270 E.G. Twitchett 30.01.1935
FBY2594 Bishop of Bloemfontein 15.09.1939
FBY2597 Bishop of Bloemfontein 02.01.1948
FBY2655 Susie Cull 29.12.1927
FBY2713 St John Ervine 16.10.1938
FBY2764 H.W.F. Franklin 22.08.1951
FBY2868 Humphrey Humphreys 15.07.1948
FBY2869 Humphrey Humphreys 03.11.1948
FBY3076 Edward Marsh 27.05.1941
FBY3077 Edward Marsh 18.12.1941
FBY3238 Colonel Denys Reitz 14.02.1944
FBY3465 Bishop of Lichfield 12.03.1940
FBY3478 Noel Brett Young 17.02.1950

Biannual publication of the Francis Brett Young Society

Newsletter 1 - 8 (July 1970 - December 1982)
Journal 9 - 35 (June 1983 - July 1996)

Books

Amos, W., *The Originals* (London: Jonathan Cape, 1985)

Boulton, J., and Robertson, A. (eds.) *Letters of D.H. Lawrence Vol. 3* (Cambridge: Cambridge University Press, 1984)

Cannadine, D., *This Little World* (Worcestershire Historical Society, 1982)

Chamberlain, A., *The Corporation Museum and Art Gallery* (Birmingham: Cornish, 1913)

Crunden, C., *A History of Anstey College, 1897-1972* (Sutton Coldfield: Anstey College, 1974)

Davies, N. de G., *Seven Private Tombs at Kurnah* (London: The Egypt Exploration Society, 1948)

De la Roche, M., *Ringing the Changes: An Autobiography* (London, Macmillan, 1957)

Drabble, M. (ed.), *The Oxford Companion to English Literature* (Oxford: Oxford University Press, 1995)

Hart-Davis, R., *Hugh Walpole: A Biography* (London: Macmillan, 1952)

Hassall, C., *Edward Marsh, Patron of the Arts: A Biography* (London: Longmans, 1959)

Hickman, J., *Life History* (Wolverhampton: Steens Ltd., n.d.)

Higham, D., *Literary Gent* (London: Jonathan Cape, 1978)

Hyde, F., *Blue Funnel* (Liverpool: University Press, 1956)

Jones, D., *The Royal Town of Sutton Coldfield* (Sutton Coldfield: Westwood Press, 1984)

Leclaire, J., *Un Temoin de l'Avenement de l'Angleterre Contemporaine: Francis Brett Young* (Rouen: l'Universite, 1969)

Mackenzie, M. Compton, *My Life and Times: Octave 5* (London: Chatto and Windus, 1966)

Marsh, E. (ed.), *Georgian Poetry 1920-1922* (London: Poetry Bookshop, 1922) [GP]

Millin, S., *General Smuts* (London: Faber & Faber, 1936)

Money, J., *Capri, Island of Pleasure* (London: Hamish Hamilton, 1986)

Ousby, I. (ed.), *The Cambridge Guide to Literature in English* (Cambridge: Cambridge University Press, 1992)

Pevsner, N., *The Buildings of England: Worcestershire* (London: Penguin, 1968)

Pooler, H., *My Life in General Practice* (London: Christopher Johnson, 1948)

Salmon, M., *Epsom College, 1855-1980: The First 125 Years* (Epsom: The College, 1980)

Schwarz, H. & L., *The Halesowen Story* (Hales Owen: H. Parkes, 1955)

Smuts, J., *Jan Christian Smuts* (London: Cassell, 1952)

Staples, B., *Francis Brett Young: A Bibliography* (London: University of London, 1958)

Stirling, W.E. & Young, F. Brett, *Crepe de Chine: The Story of the Play* (London: Mills & Boon, 1921) [CC]

Swinnerton, F., *The Georgian Literary Scene* (London: Hutchinson, 1938)

BIBLIOGRAPHY

Thompson, T., *Epsom College Register, 1855-1954* (Oxford: Oxford University Press, 1955)

Twitchett, E., *Francis Brett Young* (London: Wishart, 1935)

Walpole, H., *Essays by Divers Hands* (Oxford: University Press, 1935) [DL - EDH]

Windle, B. & Hillhouse, W., *The Birmingham School of Medicine* (Birmingham: Hall & English, 1890)

Wood, H., *My Life of Music* (London: Gollancz, 1938)

Young, F. Brett

    1. Novels

    Undergrowth (with Young, E. Brett) (London: Martin Secker, 1913) [U]

    Deep Sea (London: Martin Secker, 1914) [DS]

    The Dark Tower (London: Martin Secker, 1915) [DT]

    The Iron Age (London: Martin Secker, 1916) [IA]

    The Crescent Moon (London: Martin Secker, 1918) [CM]

    The Young Physician (London: Collins, 1919) [YP]

    The Tragic Bride (London: Martin Secker, 1920) [TB]

    The Black Diamond (London: Collins, 1921) [BD]

    The Red Knight (London: Collins, 1921) [RK]

    Pilgrim's Rest (London: Collins, 1922) [PR]

    Woodsmoke (London: Collins, 1924) [WS]

    Cold Harbour (London: Collins, 1924) [CHa]

    Sea Horses (London: Cassell, 1925) [SH]

    Portrait of Clare (London: Heinemann, 1927) [PC]

    The Key of Life (London: Heinemann, 1928) [KL]

    My Brother Jonathan (London: Heinemann, 1928) [MBJ]

    Black Roses (London, Heinemann, 1929) [BR]

    Jim Redlake (London: Heinemann, 1930) [JR]

    Mr & Mrs Pennington (London: Heinemann, 1931) [MMP]

    The House Under The Water (London: Heinemann, 1932) [HUW]

    This Little World (London: Heinemann, 1934) [TLW]

    White Ladies (London: Heinemann, 1935) [WL]

    Far Forest (London: Heinemann, 1936) [FF]

    They Seek A Country (London: Heinemann, 1937) [SC]

    Portrait of a Village (London: Heinemann, 1937) [PV]

    Dr Bradley Remembers (London: Heinemann, 1938) [DBR]

    The City of Gold (London: Heinemann, 1939) [CG]

    Mr Lucton's Freedom (London: Heinemann, 1940) [MLF]

    A Man About the House (London: Heinemann, 1942) [MAH]

    Wistanslow (London: Heinemann, 1956) [W]

    2. Short Stories

    Blood Oranges (London: White Owl Press, 1932) [BOr]

    The Cage Bird (London: Heinemann, 1933) [CB]

The Christmas Box (London: Heinemann, 1938) [CBox]
Cotswold Honey (London: Heinemann, 1940) [CHo]

3. Non-Fiction
Robert Bridges: A Critical Study (with Young, E. Brett) (London: Martin
 Secker, 1914) [RB]
Marching on Tanga (London: Collins, 1917) [MT]
In South Africa (London: Heinemann, 1952) [ISA]

4. Poetry
Five Degrees South (London: Martin Secker, 1917) [FDS]
Poems 1916-1918 (London: Collins, 1919) [P]
The Island (London: Heinemann, 1944) [I]

5. Drama
Captain Swing (with Stirling, W.E.) (London: Collins, 1919) [CS]
The Furnace (with Armstrong, W.) (London, Heinemann, 1928) [F]

6. Music
Songs of Robert Bridges (London: Breitkopf & Hartel, 1912) [SRB]
Songs for Voice and Pianoforte (London: Weeks & Co., 1913) [SVP]

7. Miscellaneous
'More Unwritten Reminiscences of Capri', *Vanity Fair*, June 1929
 [MURC - VF]
'The Secret History of a Novelist', *Good Housekeeping*, May 1935
 [SHN - GH]
'Saving the Malvern Hills', *The Times*, 16.10.1937 [T]
Young, J. Brett, *Francis Brett Young: A Biography* (London, Heinemann, 1962)

Appendix One:
Dramatis Personae

Francis Brett Young created hundreds of fictional characters. The following are used to tell his own story in this biography.

Abberley, Richard: subaltern wounded in Zulu War: CG

Achmet: Cairo dragoman: 'Glamour': CB

Ah Qui: Captain Glanvil's steward: SH; Singapore opium dealer: CM

Allbright, Madame: dress-shop owner: MMP

Altrincham-Harris, (Dr) James/Charles: G.P. (Lower Sparkdale): YP; MMP; (Mawne Heath): DBR

Barradale Mr: Engineer of North Bromwich water scheme: U; HUW

Bernstein, Leon: hero: 'Enemy Alien': CHo

Bezuidenhout, Hendrik: anthropologist: KL

Bothma, Jan; Stephanus: Boer activists: TSC

Boyce, Matthew: North Bromwich medic: YP; MBJ

Bradley (Dr) John; Matt; Matthew: hero; father; son: DBR

Bredon, Hugh: hero: KL

Bryden, Robert: hero: RK

Bulgin, John: Managing Director, Bulgin's Tube Works: MMP

Bunt, Aaron: poacher: TLW

Burwarton, Eva; (Rev.) James: heroine; brother: CM; (appeared as children: YP)

Cantlow, Jabez: Monk's Norton shopkeeper: PV

Cleaver, Mr: St Luke's schoolmaster: YP

Collins, George: Monk's Norton farmer: PV; DBR; CBox

Considine, (Rev.) Marmaduke: married Gabrielle Hewish: TB

Cookson, George: farmer at Chaddesbourne D'Abitot: TLW; BD

Craig, (Dr) Charles: Wednesford Medical Officer: MBJ

D'Abitot, Drogo: confidence trickster: 'True Blue': CHo

Dakers, Eugene; Harold; Jonathan: father; brother; hero: MBJ; (Eugene: W; Harold: DBR; W; Jonathan: DBR)

Darnay, (Fr) Cyril: Anglo-Catholic priest: PC; W

De Mathon, John: Benedictine monk of Worcester: I

Dench, (Sir) Benjamin: doctor friend

of Agnes and Ellen Isit: MAH

Downton, Sammy: St Luke's organist: YP

Essex, Colonel: i/c Second Kalahari Rifles: JR

Eve, Gunner: construction gang foreman: U; YP; BD

Fellows, Abner; John: hero; father: BD

Fladburn, Henry: son of North Bromwich Liberal Nonconformist family: WL

Folliott, John: friend of Richard Verdon, son of Viscount Crowle: W

Follows, Rev.: Rector of Monk's Norton: PV

Folville, Cynthia: daughter of Lord Essendine: JR

Fowler: butler at Alvaston Grange: MLF

Furnival, Humphrey; Jane: sinister hero; wife: CHa; (DBR); (Humphrey: PC; MBJ; HUW)

Garside, Budge: prize-fighter: BD; MMP

Glanvil, (Captain) George: hero: SH

Godovius, Herr: plantation-owner: CM

Grafton, John; Piet: English settler in South Africa; son: CG; TSC

Griffin: schoolboy bully of Edwin Ingleby, later North Bromwich student: YP

Grosmont, Alaric; Charlie; Judith: hero; brother; sister-in-law: DT; (Alaric: YP; PC)

Hadley, Aaron; George; Jenny (later Badger): chain-maker; son; daughter: FF

Hammond, (Dr) John: Wednesford G.P., partner of Jonathan Dakers: MBJ

Haskard, (Dr) Charles: North Bromwich G.P.: MMP

Hayman, Jack: hero: PR

Heal, Tommy: St Luke's mathematics teacher: YP

Hendry/Hendrie, Dr: G.P. at Lesswardine/Trewern/Chapel Green: BD; KL; JR; MMP

Hendry Mr: First Mate on *Vega/Chusan*: SH; 'The Ship's Surgeon's Yarn': CHo

Henshall, Reuben; Ruth: hero; wife: DS

Hewish, Gabrielle; Jocelyn: heroine; father: TB

Hingston, (Sir) Joseph (Lord Wolverbury): industrialist: IA; YP; CHa; PC; MBJ; MMP; HUW; TLW; WL; DBR; MLF; W

Hingston, Ralph: son of Joseph, husband of Clare: PC: MBJ; HUW; DBR; W

Hingston, Steven: son of Ralph and Clare: PC

Holly, Rev.: Vicar of Rossington: JR

Hopkins, Bert: Wednesford rambler: MLF

Ingleby, Beatrice; Edwin; John: mother; hero; father: YP; (Edwin: PC; MBJ; John: IA; BD; PC; MBJ)

Isit, Agnes; Ellen: joint heroines: MAH; (PC)

Jackson, Agatha; Simeon: heroine; husband: 'Glamour': CB

Jessell, Miss: Matron of Wednesford Cottage Hospital: MBJ

Jewell, Rev.: Vicar of Thorpe Folville: JR

Joyce, Biddy: housekeeper to Sir Jocelyn Hewish: TB

Kelly, Mr: Headmaster Halesby Grammar School: IA; YP

Kenar, Jeffrey; Nesta: disabled fisherman; wife: DS

Kington, Harry: played for Hay-on-Wye in village cricket match: MLF

Lacey, Martin: North Bromwich medic: DBR

Ledwyche, Viscount: fiancé of Helena Pomfret: 'Eros and Psyche': CB

Leeming, Mr: St Luke's Upper Fourth form master: YP

Levison, Harry: nephew of Solomon Magnus: MMP

Lingen, Canon; Charles: Rector of Temple Folliott; son: W; (Charles: HUW)

Loach, (Miss) Laura: permanent and inquisitive invalid of Chaddesbourne: TLW; PV

Longmead, Mr: Manager, Edmonsons', wholesale druggists: MBJ

Lucton, Muriel; Owen: wife; hero: MLF

Lydiatt, Ambrose; Clare (later Hingston, Wilburn): father; heroine: PC; (Clare: MBJ; HUW; MLF)

MacDiarmid: one-armed elephant-hunter: JR

Magnus, Solomon: North Bromwich stockbroker: MMP; HUW

Malcolm, (Dr) Henry: hero: 'A Busman's Holiday': CB

Malpas, Gladys; Mary (née Condover); Morgan: daughter; mother; son of Chapel Green: BD; MMP; MLF

Malthus, Catherine; Rev.: daughter; Vicar of Cold Orton: JR

Maples, Mrs: invalid neighbour of the Penningtons: MMP

Martin, Denis: North Bromwich medic: YP; MBJ

Martock, Arthur: son of Halesby

doctor: MBJ; JR; MMP

Martyn, Edie: of Silver Street, married Jonathan Dakers: MBJ; (appeared as child: DBR)

Marx, Mr: Naples shipping agent: SH

Massa, Enrico: Trinacrian revolutionary: RK

M'Crae, Hector (alias Charles Hare): one-armed elephant-hunter: CM

Medhurst, (Dr) Jacob: North Bromwich G.P., employed John Bradley: DBR

Meninsky, Isaac: pedlar and entrepeneur: CG

Monaghan, Dr: Wednesford partner of Dr Craig: MBJ

Moon, Dr Robert: North Bromwich anatomy lecturer: YP

Moore, Lloyd: North Bromwich house surgeon: YP; CHa; PC; MBJ: DBR

Morgan, Ruth: heroine: KL

Morris, Mr ('Nosey'): friend of Harry Levison: MMP

Mortimer, Bella; Harriet; Jasper: mother; aunt; grandfather of heroine: WL

Moule, Thirza: hypocritical aunt of Jenny Hadley and David Wilden: FF

Munslow, George; Laura: Landlord of Cock and Magpie; daughter: DBR

Murphy, Virginia: American artist resident in Monfalcone: MAH

Ombersley, Catherine; Helen; Miles; Richard; Roger; Jack: daughter; wife; hero; sons: TLW; (Roger: CBox)

Pearson, (Rev.) Charles: Rector of Halesby: MMP

Pennington, Dick; Judith; Susan

(née Lorimer): hero; aunt; wife:
MMP

Perkins, Jim: played for Norton
Lacey in village cricket match:
MLF

Pomfret, Helena: heroine: 'Eros and
Psyche': CB

Pomfret, Bella (née Small, Tinsley);
Hugo; Jasper: heroine; husband;
son: WL

Pomfret, Rev.: Vicar of Wychbury:
PC; MBJ; HUW; TLW; WL

Potts, John: hero: 'True Blue': CHo

Powys, Diana: daughter of Lord
Clun: MLF

Prinsloo, Adrian; Jacoba: Boer farmer
and voortreker; wife: TSC

Radway, Lieutenant: naval sub-
lieutenant serving on *Pennant*: TB

Redlake, Elizabeth; George; Jim:
father; mother; hero: JR; (Jim:
MMP)

Ritchie, Paul: hero: BR

Robinson, Mrs Louisa: Capri artist:
WL

Rudge, Mr: Monk's Norton farmer:
PV

Sanders, Mary: daughter of Aaron
Sanders of Sedgebury: DBR

Selby, Dr: Chaddesbourne G.P.:
TLW

Shellis, (Captain) Benjie: hero:
'Shellis's Reef': CB

Shelton, Bill: Worcester taverner: I

Shelton: gamekeeper: WL

Silley, Mr: fish-buyer and Methodist
preacher: DS

Small, (Captain) Joe: disabled First
World War soldier: MMP

Small, Rupert: eloped with Bella
Mortimer, father of Bella (Pomfret): WL

Spettigue, Mrs: pillar of Capri establishment: WL; 'True Blue': CHo

Stafford, Celia (née Malpas); Charles:
wife; engineer: IA; BD (Celia: FF;
Charles: WL)

Tinsley, Josiah: founder of
Hayseech Brickworks: WL

Tregaron, Gerald; Griffith; Rob;
Virginia: son; hero; son; daughter:
HUW; (Griffith: TLW; WL; Rob:
TLW; MLF)

Twiss, Mr: Chief Engineer aboard
SS Chusan: 'Shellis's Reef': CB

Verdon, Dr; Mrs; Richard: father;
mother; hero: W

Walcot, Ludlow: hero: 'Mr Walcot
Goes Home': CB

Weir, Catherine; Dr; Sylvia: aunt;
grandfather; mother of heroine:
PC; (Catherine: HUW)

Weldon, (Sir) Arthur: North Bromwich consultant physician: YP;
KL; HUW; W

Weston, (Dr) John; Jane: grandparents of Jim Redlake: JR

Widdup: schoolboy friend of Edwin
Ingleby: YP

Wiener, Louis; Otto: son; father
South African financiers: HUW

Wilburn, Dudley; Ernest: North
Bromwich solicitors: DT; PC;
MBJ; MMP; WL; MLF; MAH;
(Dudley: HUW; TLW)

Wilden, Adam; David: grandfather;
cousin of heroine: FF

Willis, Edward; Rose; Walter: son;
wife; industrialist: IA; YP; PC;
MBJ; WL; (Edward: BD; DBR;
MLF; Walter: BD; CHa; MMP;
HUW; TLW; DBR; W)

Willoughby, Kate: heroine: 'Egeria':
CB

Wills, Dr: Mawne Heath G.P.: DBR

Acknowledgements

Since John Powell Ward invited me to write this biography, many people have offered enthusiastic and willing guidance. I am particularly indebted to Alan Rankin and Brian Staples for their knowledge of Brett Young's published works and to Jack Haden, Joe Hunt and Gilian Maddison for help with the photographs.

I wish to express my gratitude to Douglas Bridgewater for information about Selby Phipson; David Eades for information about Hales Owen Magistrate's Court; Catherine Hall for bibliographical research; Vera Harber for her recollections of life at Craycombe House; Valda Napier for assistance with research in South Africa; Lena Schwarz for information concerning Brett Young's Hales Owen; Dr Rosemary Sheppard for her expert knowledge of diabetes.

Frankie Calland, Anstey Association; Pippa Hyde and Ann Stallard, Council for the Protection of Rural England; Lorraine Henderson, RNIB; R.A. David, Friends of Tewkesbury Abbey; Barbara Plant, Friends of Worcester Cathedral; Christine Penney and staff of Special Collections, University of Birmingham Library; Dr M.L. Bierbrier, British Museum; Lt Col Anthony Mather, Central Chancery of the Orders of Knighthood; Anne Kotze, Church of the Province of South Africa; City of Birmingham Reference Library; Brierley Hill Library; Dudley Archives; Library of Congress; South African Library; Merseyside Maritime Museum; National Maritime Museum, Greenwich; National English Literary Museum, Grahamstown have all provided valuable information, for which I am grateful.

Quotations from the writings of Francis Brett Young are included by permission of the University of Birmingham, the Brett Young Estate and David Higham Associates.

Series Afterword

The Border country is that region between England and Wales which is upland and lowland, both and neither. Centuries ago kings and barons fought over these Marches without their national allegiance ever being settled. It is beautiful, gentle, intriguing, and often surprising. It displays majestic landscapes, which show a lot, and hide some more. People now walk it, poke into its cathedrals and bookshops, and fly over or hang-glide from its mountains, yet its mystery remains.

The subjects covered in the present series seem united by a particular kind of vision. Writers as diverse as Mary Webb, Dennis Potter and Thomas Traherne, painters and composers such as David Jones and Edward Elgar, and writers on the Welsh side such as Henry Vaughan and Arthur Machen, bear the one imprint of border woods, rivers, villages and hills. This vision is set in a special light, a cloudy, golden twilight so characteristic of the region. As you approach the border you feel it. Suddenly you are in that finally elusive terrain, looking up from a bare height down on to a plain, or from the lower land up to a gap in the hills, and you want to explore it, maybe not to return.

There are more earthly aspects. From England the border meant romantic escape or colonial appropriation; from Wales it was roads to London, education or employment. Boundaries are necessarily political. Much is shared, yet different languages are spoken, in more than one sense. The series authors reflect the diversity of their subjects. They are specialists or academics; critics or biographers; poets or musicians themselves; or ordinary people with however an established reputation of writing imaginatively and directly about what moves them. They are of various ages, both sexes, Welsh and English, border people themselves or from further afield.

Francis Brett Young wrote about these matters from the English side. He lived variously elsewhere, in Cumbria, Devon, Africa and the Isle of Capri. Yet he was a West Midlander from the Black Country, and in his series of 'Mercian' novels and sometimes elsewhere, he made long thrusts into the Radnor heartland, coupling a robust historical and human sense with his own love of nature, hills and (near-compulsively) water. Michael Hall's uniquely authoritative knowledge of Brett Young probes this story exhaustively.

John Powell Ward

Index

About the Author

Michael Hall lives in Hales Owen, Francis Brett Young's birthplace, and is a retired Deputy Head Teacher. Vice Chairman of the Francis Brett Young Society, he has edited the teaching pack 'Francis Brett Young — Novelist of the Midlands', and wrote and presented the video *Francis Brett Young's Black Country*. He is also the author of several books of local history.